Eyes in the Night

Eyes in the Night

An Untold Zulu Story

Nomavenda Mathiane

Author's note: Recording oral history is full of challenges, particularly with regard to the accuracy of historical fact. I have tried to reconcile the oral stories with the dates, names and places in formal historical accounts but some inconsistencies have been impossible to resolve completely because the people in the story are no longer around to verify their memories. I hope this doesn't detract from your reading.

ISBN: 978-1-928257-24-0
e-ISBN: 978-1-928257-25-7

First edition, first impression 2016

Published by Bookstorm (Pty) Ltd
PO Box 4532
Northcliff 2115
Johannesburg
South Africa

www.bookstorm.co.za

Edited by Pam Thornley
Proofread by Kelly Norwood-Young
Cover design by publicide
Cover image by Gallo Images
Book design and typesetting by Triple M Design
Printed and bound in the USA

For Kings Cetshwayo and Dinuzulu,
who fought gallantly in defence of the Kingdom

Contents

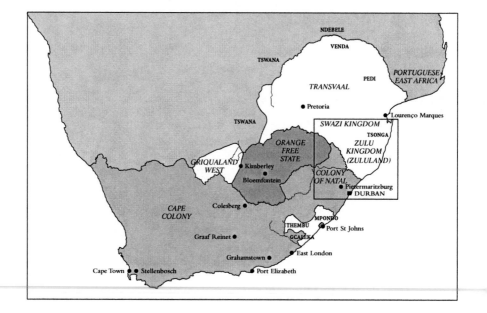

Map of southern Africa, circa 1879

Map of Zululand

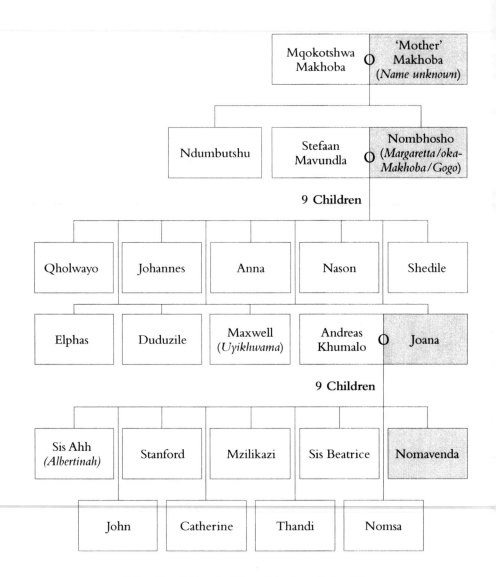

Matrilineal Family Tree of the Makhoba Clan

O = *Marriage*

Prologue

Six months before my mother died, she gave me her mother's reference book and asked me to get professionals to reconstruct the photograph in the book. She pleaded with me to take good care of it because it was the only photograph she had of her mother. I thought it odd that she should entrust me with the task because she usually assigned important duties to Mzilikazi, my older brother. I took the book from her and chucked it in one of the boxes where I keep important documents and soon forgot all about it.

My mother died in July 2003 in Qunwane, an old rural settlement in the district of Hlabisa in KwaZulu-Natal. Qunwane is a village, like many in that region, populated by people who are steeped in their traditional culture and ways; where generation after generation has been led by the Hlabisa clan and has lived in harmony for years; where a death in one family is mourned by the entire community. One of the traditions strictly observed by this community dictates that as soon as it is known that a member of the community has died, men, women and youngsters busy in their fields will stop work immediately. They will be seen on the road heading back home, carrying their hoes, picks and scythes. Nobody will work in the fields until the deceased has been buried. This practice is to honour the departed and show respect for the ground where the body is to be laid to rest.

The Sunday after Mother's funeral, when neighbours and acquaintances had left our homestead, the only people who had stayed behind apart from us, her children, were close relatives. They were there to help us with the cleaning of her house and to sort out her personal belongings.

It was a warm winter's day and we were lazing around eating the food left over from the funeral as well as conducting a post-mortem of the funeral proceedings. My brothers and sisters – there are nine of us, six girls and three boys – were sitting in my mother's dining room talking about what the speakers at the funeral had said about her. Some of the stories were hilarious while others were down-right embarrassing. One speaker told the mourners that Mother boasted about her children and the way they looked after her, that she would say she was not a chimpanzee sitting under a tree wailing. She would tell locals that she had so much money that if she laid the notes on the ground she could walk on them from her house to Nongoma, which is a stretch of about thirty kilometres. Another speaker agreed with the previous speaker, saying she had once casually asked Mother where her son Mzilikazi was teaching and her answer had been: 'Oh, that one is tired of teaching black children. He is now teaching white kids at the university.' I mean, how politically incorrect could one be? These were some of the stories with which people at her funeral service had regaled the mourners. Mother was a colourful person, full of love, song and jokes. She was ninety-seven when she died and her send-off was more of a celebration of her life than a funeral.

I was sitting next to my oldest sister Ahh this Sunday morning. Ahh is short for Albertinah. She is my mother's first-born child. Of all my mother's children, Sis Ahh is extremely laid back, soft spoken and one of the most gentle people I have ever known.

I turned to her and said: 'There is something I've never understood about Sister J.' (We called our mother Sister J, her name being Joana.) 'Do you know why she rarely spoke about her mother? For someone who used to entertain us with

2

stories of OkaBhudu (our paternal granny, her mother-in-law), there was very little she shared with us about her mom. Do you know why?'

I don't know whether or not I expected an answer. I was partly talking to myself and I was also half listening to the conversation that was taking place around the table.

'It's because her mother's story was filled with too much drama, regret, guilt and, finally, triumph. That is why she did not speak about her mom,' answered Sis Ahh.

Getting a reply from Sis Ahh surprised me. Her answer came out glibly and matter-of-factly. I paid little attention to it. And yet somehow it lingered in my mind.

The next day I drove her home and on the way I asked her what she had meant by saying our granny's story was sad and filled with drama. When we arrived at her house, she brewed a pot of tea and began her narrative. As she spoke, my mind vacillated from one emotion to the next, from sadness to anger; from a feeling of helplessness to disbelief. When she had finished talking about Grandmother's incredible tale of woe and triumph, I was filled with an overwhelming sense of pride. I was proud of the fact that I came from such ancestry.

Albertinah knew our grandmother's story because when my parents, who were officers in the Salvation Army church, were sent to do missionary work in Venda they could not take her with them because the move, which took place mid-year, would have interfered with her schooling.

They left her with Grandmother. Sis Ahh was practically raised by her. I think Ahh was ideally suited to be the one entrusted with the information. She has a calm personality and is blessed with an excellent memory. In her quiet and soft manner of speaking she recalled incidents and events that took place many years ago and related them as though they had happened yesterday. She is a retired

3

nurse and her last post was at the local hospital in Hlabisa, a facility that has become internationally renowned because of the role it has played in treating patients who are suffering from HIV and AIDS. Having trained and worked in many parts of that region she knows and understands the lie of the land and the practices of the area like no other person I know.

Sis Ahh told me her bedtime stories were never about Little Red Riding Hood and the Wolf, or about cannibals and giants. They were about the battles between the Redcoats and the various Zulu regiments. They were about our great-grandmother's survival, her unfailing support and nurture of her two young daughters and of their eking out a living on roots and rats in the caves in the Shiyane mountains; and about the final horror of witnessing corpses lying all over some of the valleys and gorges in Zululand. Even Great-grandmother's given name has sadly been lost to the ravages of time and history.

My grandmother's story, as told by Sis Ahh, solved many puzzles for me. Grandmother was a complex person with many shades to her personality. For instance, she often spoke to us in Afrikaans, especially when she was angry. But her Afrikaans was different from the one we knew and learned at school. When visiting her, this big-bosomed lady with sharp, piercing yet kind eyes would welcome us, embrace us and say, 'Kom hierso, my tjind', come here, my child. Now that is not Afrikaans as we know it. Afrikaners speak of 'kind'. She spoke Dutch.

We loved visiting Grandmother because we knew that we would be treated to good food that our parents could not afford. Her pantry was always stocked with expensive food items such as butter and cheese which she made herself. She even made her own soap. For us township children who had to buy butter from the shop, and even more so with cheese, all this was a luxury we seldom enjoyed. Only well-to-do people in the township could afford to buy expensive food items such as cheese. Grandmother had all that and more in her cupboard. I did not

4

know then that she had acquired her remarkable culinary skills during the terrifying time on the Dutch farm.

Then there was her confusing attitude towards her beliefs; she lived the latter part of her life as a devout Christian while fervently cherishing her Zulu ancestry. As a Christian, one would have expected her to exclaim, like most Christian women do: 'Oh, Jesus!' or some Christian-aligned name. Not my grandmother. She swore by King Cetshwayo. And yet, the next moment, she would, out of the blue, stand up and announce that she was going to her room to pray. She would be gone for a very long time. This dichotomy of her love for Christianity and her love for her ancestors was difficult to understand.

She was stubborn and set in her ways. For some strange reason, she could not properly pronounce the word 'holiday'. She called it 'allday'. When we tried to correct her she would say: 'I really don't care about your English because when I get to heaven God will not say, "Where are you from, Margaretta?" He will say, "Uphumaphi Nombhosho."'

After my mother's funeral, I travelled back to Johannesburg to carry on my life as a journalist. Trying to survive in Johannesburg's fast lane, I pushed my grandmother's story to the back of my mind.

Then one day I stumbled upon a book by American writer James McBride titled Song Yet Sung. *The book is about runaway slaves and slave catchers. When I had finished reading it, I knew what I had to do. I had to write my grandmother's story. I now understood why Mother had given Grandmother's reference book to me. As the journalist in the family, I was the one most suited to write the story, although I doubt Mother had the notion of my actually being inspired to write a book.*

When I realised the daunting task I had set myself, I was suddenly seized with panic. I needed to talk to Sis Ahh, as well as relatives who had at some stage lived with Grandmother. Knowing how laid-back my big sister is, I wasn't sure if she would be up to it. I also needed a photograph of my grandmother. I remembered the photograph in the reference book but I did not know where I had stashed it. I needed to find it.

Having resolved to write the book, I had to get in touch with Sis Ahh. I drove down to Zululand where I subjected my seventy-something sister to the gruelling task of remembering what Grandmother had told her around the early 1940s, about sixty years ago. Initially she didn't think much of my inquisition. She thought I was asking the questions out of curiosity, as township people are often perceived to be nosy. When I told her to think hard because I was writing a book she became reticent, and claimed she did not remember most of the stories Grandmother had told her. I suspect at that point she was regretting ever opening her mouth about this truly formidable ancestor of ours, and of how Gogo, our grandmother, had overcome one dramatic assault after another. Sis Ahh said she didn't remember some of the details of the story. At some point, she claimed to have a mental block. But I was not to be discouraged. I persisted in asking her to remember what Grandmother had told her. I asked her to close her eyes and concentrate. I really pushed her to think. The dates were the most difficult for her to remember, particularly when she had to correlate the events and the battlefields. Most of the time she got them wrong and I would ask her to think even harder. I must state here that when the dates really did not make sense to me, I would consult an independent reference source.

Initially she said our great-grandfather Makhoba, who was one of the advisers to King Cetshwayo, was killed during the Bhambatha Rebellion. I did the arithmetic and told her she was wrong. Our mother was born in late 1907 and the rebellion was in early 1906. I persuaded her to think, and think hard. One day she remembered what Grandmother had said to her about King Cetshwayo. She even sang some of the songs Grandmother had sung. The lyrics were about the life of King Cetshwayo. I also recalled one of the war songs that my mother sometimes sang which went something like 'Nasi iSangqu' (iSangqu is approaching), iSangqu being one of King Cetshwayo's regiments. The last piece of the puzzle was found. The songs were about the war between the Zulus and the English.

Having established the dates of various battles, I contacted my cousin Lillian Mjabhi Cebekhulu, née Mavundla, the daughter of one of my uncles. She too had been raised by Grandmother. She is a retired teacher who lives in Ulundi and she was a well of information. She corroborated most of what Sis Ahh had told me and added more. Between the three of us, we began our research for the book.

I plead guilty to harassing and torturing these two women, one over seventy and the other over sixty, urging them to remember the discussions they had had with Grandmother in the 1940s when they were in their teens. My worst moments were when I got a call from Sis Ahh, who suffers from diabetes, informing me that she had been hospitalised. I prayed for her return to health like I've never asked God for anything before.

An interesting dichotomy about interacting with my sister and my cousin is based on the fact that the two women are of markedly different personalities. Sis Ahh is an introvert and Mjabhi, who is much younger than Sis Ahh, is talkative, being a retired teacher. There is a commonly known story in the family that her late husband used to describe her as 'a necessary irritant'.

The two women have an indescribable love for each other and they both claim the best years of their lives were spent with Grandmother. As Mjabhi is a Mavundla, she tended to be more boastful about her heritage than Sis Ahh, who is a Khumalo. For instance, Mjabhi swore that at some point our grandfather Stefaan Mavundla visited Germany and brought back a pair of binoculars.

'Riding high on horseback, Grandpa would view the world and its people through his binoculars,' she would say. The story of Grandfather travelling overseas could not be corroborated by any of my relatives. Grandfather could have bought the binoculars in any of the shops in Vryheid or Dundee, one of my Mavundla relatives told me.

Sometimes the two women went off at a tangent, reminiscing about their stay with Grandmother and forgetting that our meeting was in fact about the book on Gogo. At times they would mix up the dates, places and battles. At worst, they contradicted each other. At such times, my journalism training would come in handy. I would rephrase my question by referring to something which they thought was totally unrelated, and that would prick their memories.

Sis Ahh's and Mjabhi's recollections helped me not only with the writing of the book but gave me a new perspective on my mother's people, the Mavundlas, the Mthiyanes. Their anecdotes reminded me of some of the stories that Mother had told us about her home and the type of man her father was. To us Grandpapa, whose name was Stefaan (Steven – he was baptised by the Lutheran clergy), was fondly called Mvangeli, which meant preacher. He was dark with chubby cheeks boasting of very deep dimples, something that most of his daughters and granddaughters inherited. He was a jolly old man who loved singing. He taught us songs and told funny stories. Long before we could speak SeSotho, Grandpa told us he could speak the language. When we asked him to say a few words in SeSotho, he replied, 'Kim kim, ke reya.' We were impressed. But later in life we discovered that he was teasing us; he did not know a word of SeSotho.

The story of my grandmother as told to me by Sis Ahh and Mjabhi put into context the relevance of my mother's reference to the many important people who visited her home in Isikhwebezi in Northern Zululand, where they spent a great deal of time talking to her father.

Each time she read of important Zulu politicians in the Ilanga lase Natal *newspaper — a weekly periodical that has outlived most African-owned publications, founded by John Langalibalele Dube in 1903 and written in IsiZulu — Mother would tell us how some of these personalities had visited her home to seek counsel with her father. She often spoke of outstanding politicians such as John Dube and Pixley Isaka ka Seme. I remember her saying that a special ilawu (hut) had been set aside at her home in Isikhwebezi for the use of King Solomon ka Dinuzulu, who was a frequent visitor to her home. Being township children, the names Mother was dropping meant nothing to us. We knew only of the Mandelas, the Sobukwes and the Sisulus. Besides, at that age we had little interest in matters that dealt with Zulu royalty.*

Sis Ahh's and Cousin Mjabhi's narratives helped me connect the dots, and what I came up with astounded me. I began to understand the kind of problems people of that era were grappling with. I was exposed to knowledge and insights that I would never have found in any classroom or textbook. I began to respect my grandparents even more, appreciating the quiet role they played in shaping the history of the region. I also began to value African people's experiences as the harsh 'wind of change' raged through southern Africa.

Sis Ahh's homestead is high on a hill. It is made up of many houses. Someone unfamiliar with the area can walk past this residence without giving it a second glance because the entire place is surrounded by trees. Once in the yard, one may easily get lost manoeuvring one's way between the houses, some built in modern rural architecture of brick and roofed with corrugated iron or with tiles; and a few rondavels — little huts made out of grass. A motorist unfamiliar with this set-up needs to be extra careful as he negotiates the treacherous curving driveway, particularly during the rainy season when the little stretch of road becomes slippery.

Sis Ahh and I preferred working on the book sitting under the shade of the trees outside the house. I sat on the bench, leaning against the wall of the main house while Sis Ahh sat on the grass mat, swatting away the mosquitoes and the flies, those meddlesome insects that thrive in the verdant vegetation in that part of the countryside. People passing by would not have guessed that we were engrossed in the difficult task of recalling a past that we had not been a part of. In a quiet voice, almost as though she was drowsy, Sis Ahh recalled the numerous conversations she had held with our granny, who was fondly called okaMakhoba by everyone, until we could almost imagine it was Gogo herself speaking to us ...

PART ONE

A Nation Besieged

I do not know in what year I was born but I remember that I was a young girl about to reach puberty when the war between the Zulus and the English broke out.

I mention my puberty status because in those days people's birth dates were not recorded. Their ages were determined either by the development landmarks of their bodies, by plagues, or by some historical milestone.

I begin my narrative by recalling what happened in 1879, the year in which I grew up faster than I could shout my name. That year was the one in which we experienced events and encounters that no one, particularly a child, should ever witness. It was also the year my people lost everything – their land and fields – and were reduced to being vagrants and beggars in the land of their birth.

I am the daughter of Mqokotshwa Makhoba, one of King Cetshwayo's generals of the iNgobamakhosi regiment, who was later elevated to the status of adviser to the king. Mqokotshwa named me Nombhosho, which means bullet. He said I would come out of any situation fast and unscathed like a bullet, and he named his second and last daughter Ndumbutshu which he said was the manner in which a bullet exits the barrel of a gun.

Although I was a young girl when the war broke out I remember as if it was yesterday the political climate of the time as well as the social conditions that engulfed us in Zululand. How can I forget the war between the English and the Zulus, and about King Cetshwayo?

At times when reading the *Ilanga lase Natal* I would get angry when we were told about hundreds of people who had been bombed in Italy and in England. What about our regiments who died by the thousands? Whoever cared to write about them? Whoever highlighted the plight of our nation? We were under siege the moment the strange-looking people set foot in Zululand.

★

For a moment, a picture of my granny flashed into my mind. I was about eighteen years old when she died. Although I saw her a few times when we visited her when my parents were on holiday, her picture remained etched in my mind. I have a vivid memory of the big-busted lady who seemed larger than life. The one aspect of her looks that springs to my mind whenever I think of her is how her pinafore dresses were often chafed and discoloured around her breasts due to excessive washing around that part of her body. She always looked ever so clean, as though she had just stepped out of a bath. Although she was not what one would describe as a beauty, her facial features were captivating. For a Zulu woman, she was fairly light in complexion with high cheekbones, a small nose, piercing yet kind eyes and thin lips. She could easily have passed for Khoisan.

★

My childhood home was in the Oqongweni village in the valley next to the Shiyane mountains. We lived a stone's throw from the now world-famous Isandlwana mountain. From where we lived we could clearly see the strange-looking people who had pitched tents on the green slopes next to the mountain. There were plenty of unpalatable stories told about these strange people, whom King Shaka called abelumbi.

★

According to legend, King Shaka referred to white people as abelumbi – sorcerers – because he couldn't fathom how their artillery could harm and kill from a distance. However, over the years, the name abelumbi was bastardised to a point where whites are now referred to as abelungu – the good or the kind ones – a word whose origins have always baffled me because while I was growing up in the 1960s there were so many stories about cruelty meted out to Africans by abelungu, stories that made me wonder if these narratives were fables or legends.

★

The arrival of abelumbi on these shores gave rise to many stories. The worst rumour which was travelling fast, far and wide, which more than illustrated the treacherous ways of the foreigners, was the tale of the abduction of young Zulu women by these people. It was alleged that a group of white men on horseback had taken advantage of the absence of Zulu men who had been summoned to the king's palace at Ondini. The white men had wooed young women around the uMzinyathi area to work in their homes. They promised the women heaven on earth. The ones who consented to go with them were made to dispose of their isidwaba, the traditional hide skirt worn by Zulu women, and had to wear invaders'

15

apparel of unsightly, long flowing skirts. They also made the women shave their heads and remove the inhloko, the traditional Zulu women's head-gear, which they claimed provided a convenient habitat for lice.

When the men returned to their homes, they found their wives, lovers and sisters had gone to work for the white people. To the men who had been away meeting with the king and the nation's leaders and elders, trying to find a solution to the impasse created by the invaders, this exodus of the women was an affront, a betrayal of the nation. The men were so angry that they went after the women. When they found them they beat them to a pulp. Others were simply killed.

Soon the rumours of an impending war became a reality as wagons were seen criss-crossing the land and tents were set up sporadically in many parts of the country. We Zulu people watched in awe as animals such as horses and oxen pulled structures that seemed like little houses with men inside them. They were wagons. When not riding on the wagons or their horses, these strange-looking people could be seen in big peaked hats and red coats strutting up and down the land as if they owned it. To add pain to humiliation and uncertainty, the British Secretary for Native Affairs, Sir Theophilus Shepstone, whom the Zulu people called Somtseu, sent an ultimatum to King Cetsh-wayo instructing him to disband his regiments as well as pay a fine of five hundred cattle for failing to adhere to the terms put to him when he was crowned King of the Zulus.

When the king learned of Somtseu's demands, he fumed and swore that he would rather die than accede to them. He told his people to prepare for war.

By the end of winter a large part of the country was dotted with tents, coaches and wagons, as well as horses belonging to the invaders. It was clear to everyone that the foreigners' intentions were to annihilate us and force us off our land. It was also clear that the enemy was prepared to go to any lengths to achieve this goal.

One day the king's spies spotted a new settlement that had sprung up not far from our village Oqongweni.

That was the last straw for King Cetshwayo who immediately gave orders that we should move because he was getting ready to strike at the invaders. He had tolerated enough humiliation from them, particularly from Somtseu who was treating him as his subject and dictating to him how to rule his people. The king swore he was going to show Somtseu and the rest of the foreigners what the Zulu people were made of.

There were other white people who were also involved in the fracas like Sir Bartle Frere, the British High Commissioner for Southern Africa, and Sir Henry Bulwer, the Governor of Natal, to mention a few, but Somtseu was the one who was in our faces. He was the one who interacted directly with the king and his messengers, the one who imposed fines on King Cetshwayo. The rest of the foreigners were in the background.

There is no doubt that Shepstone was the most hated white man in Zululand. The Zulu people did not understand how a foreigner could lord it over their nation. Nobody knew who had bestowed on him, foreigner that he was, the right to dictate terms of governance to the king and his people. It was not the colour of his skin that the Zulus objected to; we just could not understand why he was meddling in our affairs.

Somtseu was not the first white person to interact with the Zulu people. There had been, in the past, numerous white people who had lived among the Zulus but none had displayed contempt for them in the way that Somtseu did. For instance, there was Henry Francis Fynn, a trader whom we called Findo. He had been trading in Zululand for years and had befriended King Shaka. The two men had a healthy relationship. Findo had learned the Zulu ways and spoke our language. Somtseu also spoke isiZulu and isiXhosa fluently, and was fully conversant with Zulu customs and traditions, yet he regarded the Zulu people with condescension. In response to his attitude, the Zulus saw him as an interloper.

I knew about Somtseu because my father who was then a member of the king's advisory team had, on behalf of the king, met Somtseu on numerous occasions, such as when he had to deliver fines in the form of cattle or elephant tusks as peace offerings or when Somtseu's emissaries delivered ultimatums to King Cetshwayo. My father was part of the delegation that received the British envoys.

The Zulu people were irked by Somtseu's discourteous omnipresence. We did not understand why he featured so prominently in our lives and why we were on the receiving end of his wrath. We could not comprehend why he was persecuting King Cetshwayo when the king had done him no wrong. If anything, it was Somtseu and his people who were the aggressors in our land.

One of the incidents for which Somtseu penalised the king for was the vengeful behaviour of some drunken Zulus who had assaulted two white men who were working on the road. The incident had occurred at the height of hostilities between the Zulus and the foreigners. The Zulu men had seen the white men in their part of the land working on the road and had confronted them. They wanted to know who had given them permission, as foreigners, to do whatever it was they were doing. When there was no explanation forthcoming from the white men, partly because of the language barrier and partly because they did not deem it necessary to explain themselves to people they perceived as inferior, the Zulus were incensed by their arrogance and beat them up.

When Somtseu was informed of the incident, he was hopping mad and he immediately sent an envoy to King Cetshwayo, fining him five hundred cattle as compensation for the assault on the two white men.

Another matter which I was convinced was one of the main causes of the war between the Zulu people and the English was the Mehlokazulu debacle. Mehlokazulu was the son of Sihayo, one of King Cetshwayo's most trusted and fearless warriors and generals. Though diminutive in stature, Sihayo was revered and popular all over Zululand and is rumoured to have had thirty-eight wives. He lived a stone's throw from Isandlwana mountain. One of his wives, okaQwelebane left him to cohabit with a man who lived beyond the Zululand border, on the side of the Boers. Like his father, Mehlokazulu was brave and fearless. When he learned of his mother's adultery and betrayal of the Zulu cause by opting to go and live with a deserter, Mehlokazulu was livid. Without his father's knowledge or approval, he decided that he was going to kill his mother to avenge his father's humiliation.

The only person Mehlokazulu confided in was his father's second wife, who, when she learned of his intentions responded by saying: 'Tell me you are joking.'

'No, I'm not joking. I am going to smash her head with this assegai and scatter her brain all over the rocky mountain,' was Mehlokazulu's reply as he embarked on his deadly mission. He was accompanied by a group of friends who were as hotheaded as he was. However, the friends didn't know that he was planning to kill his mother. They were under the impression that he intended killing his mother's lover.

The young warriors set off on their bloodthirsty journey across the border in a carefree manner, betraying no emotion about the nature of their mission. As they didn't want to be noticed or recognised by the villagers where okaQwelebane was now living, they casually picked their way amidst the low cliffs and dongas and arrived at the village just as the sun was setting. They selected a good vantage point behind the dongas of the establishment, where they could watch the activities taking place in and around the homestead where their prey was now living. They saw the boys herd the cattle back to the homesteads and milk the cows; they watched the girls return from the river carrying calabashes full of water while some were making fires on the floor hearth ready to prepare the evening meal.

The young warriors waited until the boys had concluded their daily chores and had locked the cattle in the pen before retiring into their respective huts. Surreptitiously, Mehlokazulu and his friends moved nearer the homestead. They hid among the bushes that were part of the hedge that surrounded the kraal and waited for okaQwelebane to make an appearance. They knew that she would at some stage have to respond to the call of nature. Indeed, when it became dark, they spotted her leaving the main hut and approaching the bushes in search of a place to relieve herself. As soon as she was done with her business, the men pounced on her and frogmarched her away from the homestead.

OkaQwelebane realised that she was being abducted by none other than her son. She knew how hard-hearted he was and that soon, as the isiZulu saying goes, 'the vultures would be hovering over her corpse'. She began pleading for mercy, reminding her son that she was the woman who had brought him into the world and promising that she would go back home to her husband. But her lamentations and pleas fell on deaf ears. As soon as they were away from the village, Mehlokazulu grabbed her, wrung and broke her neck, dropped her lifeless body on the ground and crossed the border back home.

Somtseu must have rubbed his hands in glee when the news reached him because he now had a valid reason to attack King Cetshwayo, claiming the king had not kept his side of the bargain by not adhering to the terms of governance.

The terms stipulated by Somtseu were that the king should disband his regiments, abstain from the practice of sniffing out witches and stop the slaying of his subjects. Somtseu sent a delegation to King Cetshwayo, demanding Mehlokazulu's head on the proverbial platter. He fined the king five hundred cattle, but not just ordinary cattle. He demanded a certain breed of cattle – the Nyonikayiphumuli breed. This was a special type of cattle that was first bred by King Shaka and from that time onwards they were bred only by royalty. To this day they are still regarded by the Zulu people as a symbol of Zulu sovereignty. They are spotless white cattle which commoners are not allowed to breed. Somtseu also demanded that the king hand over Sihayo, Mehlokazulu and his conspirators to stand trial for okaQwelebane's murder. It didn't matter to Somtseu that the crime had been committed outside Cetshwayo's jurisdiction. Somtseu wanted Zululand, and Mehlokazulu had given him a good excuse to annihilate it. But the king was not about to betray his loyal subjects. He dug in his heels and flatly refused to hand over Mehlokazulu and Sihayo.

This stand-off was to result in the outbreak of the war that took the lives of thousands of Zulu people and hundreds of English soldiers. It displaced many families and was the precursor to the destruction of the Zulu nation.

*

These events took place not long after King Cetshwayo was crowned king of the Zulu people, an occasion which Somtseu not only attended, but one in which he officiated as representative of the British monarch, Queen Victoria, and placed a tinsel crown on King Cetshwayo's head; read him the governing rights which was a long list of dos and don'ts including a direct order to Cetshwayo to disband his regiments.

Somtseu's participation in the sacred ceremony was perceived by the Zulu people as interference of the worst kind. The nation was incensed by the meddling of a foreigner in such an important national event. They did not appreciate a foreigner, who was by all accounts their adversary, crowning their king and dictating the terms of governance. However, unbeknown to Somtseu, the Zulu people had already performed their own crowning ceremony so they simply shrugged off Somtseu's performance and dismissed it as the expected antics of an outsider.

This was not the first time that whites had interfered in Zulu sovereignty. A precedent had already been set by the Boers who had installed King Mpande, King Cetshwayo's father, as king of the Zulus although the circumstances regarding King Mpande's relationship with the Boers were different from those between King Cetshwayo and the English. King Mpande had strong ties with the Boers. At the height of the war between King Dingane and the Boers, Prince Mpande had been whisked away across the border and had sought asylum with the Boers. Although this defection was seen by the Zulu people as an act of cowardice on the part of Prince Mpande, it was a political strategy. Mpande was one of King Shaka's brothers, the son of King Senzangakhona. Shaka and his brothers Dingane and Mhlangana did not have wives or offspring. Mpande, on the other hand, was the only prince who had wives and had sired children. As the war raged, it became prudent that in order to save the royal lineage, Prince Mpande be removed from the war zone because had he died at war it would have been the end of the Zulu monarchy. This defection did not sit well with King Dingane particularly because in his flight Mpande took an entire regiment with him, virtually leaving King Dingane in the lurch.

It therefore did not come as a surprise to the amaZulu when, at the end of the war, the Boers brought Mpande back to Zululand and crowned him king of the amaZulu. It was also 'payback time' for the Boers from the man they had protected against his brother. King Mpande compensated the Boers by granting them verdant land between Vryheid, Utrecht and Melmoth. Years later the area around Vryheid would become a National Party stronghold.

Is it any wonder that this is what the praise singer said about Mpande at his coronation:

UMpande, UMsimude,
owavela ngesiluba phakathi kwamaNgisi naMaqadasi.
Mpande, one who appeared hidden between the English and the Boers.

King Mpande became the longest ruler of the Zulu people, dying of old age in 1872. His son King Cetshwayo succeeded him after killing his rival half-brother Mbuyazi. Not long after King Cetshwayo ascended the throne more foreigners descended on Zululand. They pitched their tents in and around the Shiyane mountains and the uMzinyathi River. To us, it was no longer a case of 'if' we got attacked by the invaders; it was a matter of 'when' we got attacked. The herdboys were deployed to take the livestock into the mountains and the regiments assembled at KwaNodwengu, Cetshwayo's military base, and prepared for war.

The king ordered that children, women and the infirm must flee to the mountains taking with them only the bare necessities: sleeping mats and blankets as well as foodstuffs such as ground sorghum and maize and calabashes filled with fresh and sour milk. We left behind hectares and hectares of fields in which we had painstakingly toiled. We had been blessed with good rainfall that particular year and we were expecting good harvests. Already the maize looked appetising, wrapped as it was in green leaves topped with a lush beard, an indication that the cobs were almost ready to be harvested. Soon the king would have called the nation to undertake the pilgrimage to the sacred mountain to give thanks for the first fruits of the harvest. As the rain had fallen abundantly that year, the verdant hills and valleys of Zululand were overgrown with various kinds of vegetation.

The Zulu people refer to the month of December as uZibandlela, the covered pathways, because the rain falls amply during that time of the year and the grass grows quickly and wildly and covers the footpaths in the countryside. This was the time when the rivers overflowed, nurturing the indigenous vegetation growing along the river banks – the Izindoni (water berry), a dark maroon sweet fruit, the amathunduluka, a succulent red sweet and sour grapelike fruit, the amahlala (monkey apples), a tennis-ball-sized fruit resembling an apple which has large slippery pips and a hard shell. Some creative people let this fruit dry, carefully opened it up to empty out its contents and then glued back the cut piece before artistically carving its exterior to create different ornamental designs. It was a time when girls enjoyed gathering wood from the forest as they got a chance to feast on the wild fruits. It was the season when snakes came out of hibernation and inhabited the trees searching for food. All of that was left behind when we fled into the mountains.

★

We left our homes at the beginning of January, one of the hottest months of the year, and we found a cave in the Shiyane mountains that served us as a fortress. The living conditions in this hideout were unbearable. There were about fifty people crowded into a space large enough to accommodate twenty at the most. We huddled together, cousins, aunts, grandmother, my mother and my little sister sharing this limited space with our neighbours. The only saving grace of the whole experience was that, apart from the absence of my father and uncles, the Makhoba clan was still together as a family. This togetherness was to sustain and boost our spirits and helped to maintain our sanity.

Sharing the small space with our neighbours was most uncomfortable. Even though we were members of the same community and knew one another relatively well, being crammed together in this tiny space for an indefinite period of time took a toll on everybody. There was no room to manoeuvre and the lack of hygiene was a major problem. Because there were no ablution or toilet facilities, the stench in the cave was more than one could bear, particularly during the night.

These intolerable living conditions were being visited upon a people who owned large homesteads, where space had never been a problem. We came from villages where families had many huts for members of the clan. The lack of space which we experienced in the cave meant we had to sleep sitting in an upright position. Sometimes even that posture of sleeping with one's legs stretched out was impossible because there might be a sick person sleeping nearby who needed more space. It was a difficult time for people who came from homesteads where they even had huts for the hens to sleep in.

Although my immediate family was small – just father, mother, my little sister and me – we had several huts. There was a hut in which we did the cooking. This was where the calabashes of milk were stored and fresh mealies were roasted on an open fire. There was a hearth where my mother cooked the game hunted by my father. This room saw a never-ending string of people come and go. Relatives and friends dropped by to see Mother and socialise while she prepared meals for the family. It was also the room that had an ever-present stench of smoke. One didn't need to spend a great deal of time there to emerge with eyes itching, reeking of smoke from fire made of wood and dried cow dung, and added to that the smell of food.

We had a special hut for dining and entertaining, where we often shared a meal of sour milk and uphuthu. Mother prepared my father's meal and asked me to take it to him. I remember the first time she asked me to do this I was nervous, yet also thrilled. I was only knee high and

I wasn't sure if I would be able to carry the food from Mother to my father. For a moment I thought Mother was joking, that she would get up and take the food to Father herself. Then I realised she was serious about it. I took his udiwo, a small, specifically designed clay dish with an aperture covered with a small imbenge – a saucer-like contraption made out of grass that served as a lid on which was placed a wooden spoon for eating. I put the food in front of my father and curtseyed before going back to join my mother and sister who were sitting a little way away from him.

When I looked back at my father, he was smiling. With his kind approving eyes he said: 'Oh, you have grown up, girl, you can even make food for me. Thank you.'

I felt good and proud as though I had personally prepared the food for him. From that day onwards I was the one who served him his food. When he had finished eating, he would call me to remove the udiwo and every time, without fail, he would leave some food for me. Because I was not supposed to use my father's eating utensils, I would empty the food into my bowl and invite my sister to join me in having our father's leftovers.

Then there was the bedroom which stood alone, apart from the rest of the huts. There was a special hut for visitors, fully stocked with grass mats and blankets hanging on the wall. There was the important hut for storing food, where tons of dry mealies and sorghum were kept; where meat from a slaughtered beast was hung high up on the wooden beam that held the grass hut together so that the blood could drain from the carcass.

My uncles had even more huts because their families were larger. My

cousins, girls and boys, had their own huts where they slept and entertained their friends.

Now we were living on the mountain. To us children, life in the
cave was fun as well as confusing. It was fun because we didn't have to
perform tedious domestic chores such as fetching water from the river
or collecting firewood from the forest. Without chores to perform, we
idled day in and day out, eating the little food available, telling each
other stories and sleeping. The confusing part of living on the mountain
was that we did not understand why we had to leave our homes and
lead this nomadic life. And nor did we understand why we were being
hunted like animals.

The sleeping arrangements on the mountain were simple. The girls
and the babies slept in one corner, the women in another corner and
the old and infirm gathered in their own little nook. There were discussions about the war day and night. Some of the old people suffered from
insomnia and talked right through the night.

It happened often that one would wake up in the middle of the
night to the sounds of heated arguments among the war veterans
who were sharing the cave with us. These were the old men who had
been part of King Shaka's army as young boys, deployed to carry war
paraphernalia and food supplies for the warriors. They had interacted
with revered warriors who formed King Shaka's gallant regiments of
amaPhela and Ombelebele. They had not only survived King Shaka's
many battles and skirmishes, but had later fought in battles like Blood
River, where thousands of Zulu warriors had died like flies at the
hands of the Boers. These men had been the bricks of the Zulu nation
and were the glue that had held the nation together. The wise, brave

old men talked about the good old days when King Shaka was in charge of the country and had instilled a sense of pride and bravery in his subjects. They were proud of their customs and traditions, and their heritage.

They argued among themselves about which regiment should have been deployed at what point and why, and they were often critical of King Cetshwayo's generals and their war strategies. They openly longed for the days when they were young boys, watching Shaka's regiments engaging in the renowned head and horns battle formation.

The old people in the cave reminisced at length about the days when the land was under Shaka's rule. They argued that although it was a time when the nation was embroiled in endless battles and numerous unwarranted deaths, it was also a time when people led a relatively bountiful life, when there was plenty to eat and to live on, when every household had cattle and goats and hectares of land to plough. They compared King Dingane's reign with that of King Shaka and agreed that the differences were glaring. While they acknowledged the hardships they had experienced during the reign of Shaka, they also confessed to the realisation that he had been a unique leader, endowed with remarkable intelligence and vision.

They recounted anecdotes to illustrate his qualities. Some of these stories are now legends, such as the one of a white trader who, when King Shaka complained of a headache, offered him a bottle of painkillers, and told him to take two. King Shaka, who was suspicious of abelumbi, gave the bottle of pills back to the trader and demanded that he should swallow all the pills to prove that they were effective. King Shaka was believed to be a visionary and examples were given to support their narratives. One conversation often repeated was of King Shaka asking a white visitor how many kings there were in Europe. The man told him that there were many kings. King Shaka responded by advising the man to go back to Europe and kill all the monarchs so that he should rule over the white people in Europe and King Shaka would annihilate all the kings in Africa and the two would rule the world.

The old people conceded that they had initially viewed King Dingane, who succeeded King Shaka, as a liberator. His reign had been relatively easy-going – he was a king who loved the good life, song and dance – until he plunged the nation into a war with the Boers in an attempt to stop the strangers from settling in Zululand.

The old warriors shook their heads in dismay when talking about the aftermath of that war, which saw people abducted by the invaders and turned into slaves. Others willingly went to the Boers because they could not cope with life after having lost everything they owned.

The old warriors despised the weak people who had capitulated to the foreigners and had become white people's property. The concept of someone working for anyone other than the king was alien and repulsive to the veterans in the cave. As warriors they had been in many skirmishes with the neighbouring clans and had brought prisoners from these wars back to the king. The vanquished warriors were not killed unless they displayed tendencies of arrogance towards the victors. But once they had accepted their status of being defeated, and were willing to be part of the Zulu nation, they were treated like any other person who swore allegiance to the king. They led normal lives as heads of their families, dividing their time between their homesteads and the king's court. The women who had lost husbands in the war were taken on as wives by the warriors. The transition from enemy to being part of the Zulu nation was made easy because the warring parties were from the Nguni clans; they spoke the same language and practised similar customs and traditions to the Zulu people.

The old people harboured fears for the future. Although we were living in the shadow of death, they did not fear dying; if anything, they expressed a longing for it. To them, death was a better option than a future under the invaders. They spoke fondly of how death would reunite them with their long-departed relatives and friends who were awaiting their arrival in the afterlife. To them, the future was so uncertain that whenever they broached the question of surviving the war, fear was visible in their eyes.

They were not the only ones who were worried about the future; we all were. It was obvious to everyone living on the mountain that life after the war would never be the same.

As the young and able-bodied men were locked in battle with the foreigners, the women and children, the old and the sick were wrestling with the question of what would happen to the nation once the war was over. We knew we could not live in the mountains and dongas for ever. One day, the war would be over and we would have to come down from the mountain. What kind of life would await us?

We also knew that if we won the war it would be only a matter of time before the invaders reorganised themselves and struck again. Hadn't we thought the war was over when so many of our people were killed by the Boers at the Ncome River? Did the outcome of that battle not result in the Boers taking a large part of our land and our cattle? Whether or not we won this war, the invaders had made it clear they were fighting us in order to seize the rest of the land and turn us into their slaves. Whatever the outcome of the war, nothing was going to change the fact that we were a besieged nation.

★

As we spent days and nights in the belly of the mountain warriors from the battle front would sometimes come to the cave to check on the members of their families. They updated us on the progress of the war. We got to know who had been killed as well as learned of the damage inflicted on the foe. Whichever way the battle was going, the young warriors were convinced that ultimately they would win the war. They were not discouraged by the fact that their archaic artillery was inflicting little damage on an enemy using modern and sophisticated armoury. They believed in King Cetshwayo who had instilled a pride of the Zulu prowess and the need to fight for their land. As in the time of King Shaka, his regiments engaged in the much-acclaimed horns and head battle formation.

We were still living in the caves when the news reached us that our regiments had ambushed the invaders. A battle was fought in the early hours of the morning at the foot of the mountain aptly called Isandlwana, which means the mountain that looks like a hut. Our regiments had annihilated the invaders to the point where the few who had survived had made no attempt to retaliate but had fled.

When the king learned of the victory at Isandlwana he slaughtered many cattle and the nation celebrated. However, the euphoria of the regiments' success was short lived because the warriors ignored the king's instructions not to venture into the areas where the enemy had bivouacked. Driven by the adrenalin of success, the regiments gave chase to the enemy up to Rorke's Drift, previously a trading station built on a plateau not far from Isandlwana whose buildings had been transformed into war barracks to accommodate the soldiers, war paraphernalia and foodstuffs. It was also a makeshift hospital.

When our warriors got to Rorke's Drift, they were greeted by a volley of bullets and gunfire. Thousands were killed and from that day on the fortunes of the Zulu nation were to take a nosedive heralding the beginning of the destruction of the Zulu empire.

After the battle at Rorke's Drift the enemy began advancing towards where we were hiding. With the enemy having been sighted nearby, everyone had to vacate this part of the mountain.

One morning Father arrived at the cave and told us we were no longer safe where we were. He was moving us, his immediate family only, to another part of the mountain. He said this was a precautionary measure. He didn't want the Makhoba clan located in one place in case of an attack. He said my uncles would be coming for the rest of the family.

We were then separated from the rest of the group, from my aunts and cousins and grandmother. They were to find another hideout. Father later told me that as much as he would have loved to have taken his mother with us he could not because the person who was responsible for Grandmother's upkeep was the oldest member of the family and that was Makhoba Omkhulu. My father was the youngest of the lot.

We parted from members of our family and from some of our neighbours. They did not know where we were going and nor did we know

33

where they would be going to hide. With tears cascading down my cheeks, I kissed my aunts and cousins goodbye. The worst moment was when I had to bid farewell to my grandmother. The war had taken its toll on her. She had aged beyond her years and looked frail and weak from worry and lack of good food. Three of her sons were at the battlefields and now she was to part from us. We said our teary farewells and father led the way.

I walked away wondering if I would ever see my dear relatives again. Taking my sister's hand, I followed my parents. Occasionally I'd look back to catch a glimpse of the mountain housing the members of my family whom I had left behind. Gradually, as I looked back, the mountain seemed to fade away. And soon it had disappeared into the sunset.

We walked the whole day and arrived at the cave in the evening. Along the way we had dug up roots that we planned to have for supper but by the time we arrived at our destination we were too tired to eat anything. Once we had cleared the cave of dirt and made sure that it was habitable, we settled in for the night. For the first time in many weeks Father spent the night with us. But he was gone with the first ray of dawn. He had gone back to the king's palace at Ondini and we were once more left to fend for ourselves.

If living in our first hideout had been unbearable, living in the new cave was worse. We were alone, my mother, my little sister and I. Except for rare visits from my father, we were completely isolated from the world. We did not even know the name of the mountain where we were hiding, let alone what the area was called. We spent days wondering what was happening at the war front. Mother spent most of the time in silence and was emotionally absent. She seemed to be in a perpetually pensive mood. At times I would hear her singing a tune which alluded to King Cetshwayo's persecution:

Bayamqala okaNdaba,
Yena uzithulele, akaqali muntu;
Bayamqala okaNdaba.
They are provoking the great one,
Yet he is quiet and not retaliating;
They are provoking the great one.

She sang this melancholy song for hours, slowly rocking her torso backwards and forwards as she sang. Sometimes she would hum it. When she did that, I often saw tears streaming down her cheeks. Added to her meditative and seemingly absent state of mind, she also faced the ordeal of having to deal with the inquisitive mind of a ten-year-old. I wanted to know why we were forced to live in caves like animals. I had had enough of the rough life. I longed for my home and all the comforts it provided. I asked her numerous questions. She could not adequately explain to me why the foreigners were chasing and killing us. She could not tell me what wrong we had committed to be condemned to losing our homes and our possessions.

'My child,' she said, 'these are difficult times. We are living in the wilderness because of the invasion by strange people who want to eliminate the Zulu nation, but I can tell you they will not succeed. The king and our regiments will fight to the bitter end to protect us and our land. I assure you, we will triumph over this.'

Sometimes in the dead of night Mother talked to herself although she was obviously addressing me. It was as though she was preparing me for the hard times that lay ahead. I would wake up to hear her dishing out advice to me and my sister.

'One day you girls will be grown up and will become mothers. I want you to know that it is important that you behave well and show respect. You must respect your elders, your leaders, the earth where our food comes from and the animals that provide us with milk and meat. And, more importantly, you must respect who you are and your ancestors. Always remember you come from good and proud people.'

At such times she would also talk to me about the responsibilities of being a girl and tell me about the changes my body would undergo as I grew up.

'I may not have a broom to swat the two pimples when they appear on your breast, but I promise you, I will use these leaves on your chest and I swear by Cetshwayo that they will disappear,' she said. There was a strong belief among Zulu women that the development of breasts on teenagers could be delayed or halted by swatting the chest with a hand broom made of grass.

'But Ma,' I argued, 'I also want to grow breasts. Some of my friends have them.'

We engaged in long discussions about what would happen to my body when I grew up. At times I would wake up at night to feel her hands tenderly scratching my head, checking to see if there were any lice in my hair because we hadn't washed in months.

Sometimes we talked for a long time. I argued with her, telling her that she should stop thinking that we would one day leave the mountain. I was convinced that we were doomed to live there for ever. But she thought differently. She believed that the king and the regiments would liberate us and we would return to our wonderful life in the valleys of the Shiyane mountains where the uMzinyathi River flowed incessantly.

On our journey to the mountain we had seen many villages that had been deserted. Some had been burnt down. We had come across corpses lying on the paths. They were the bodies of warriors sprawled on the ground with their spears next to them. Some lay with their eyes and mouths open, with flies hovering all over their bodies. In other cases, the vultures were already at work. We had also seen corpses of women and children. It was as if someone had been going about the valley discarding the dead at random, like throwing mealies at chickens. There was no pattern or order to the corpses lying along the paths. In the beginning when we encountered the dead bodies we chased the vultures away and buried the dead in shallow graves. But soon there was no time to conduct burials as the enemy was on our heels. There also came a time when we did not have the energy to chase away the vultures feeding on the dead or hovering on the horizon. We were weak and emaciated from lack of food. We were almost like corpses ourselves and I suspect the vultures were aware of our weak physical condition and were biding their time knowing we could drop dead any minute.

We were now living in this tiny cave. We didn't know where the rest of our family was and I missed my extended family and the happy days we had led at the large Makhoba homestead. I missed my uncles. My father was the youngest of three brothers. My oldest uncle, Makhoba Omkhulu, was the gentlest of the three. Although he was a brave warrior belonging to uFalaza regiment, he was more at home with his cattle and dogs. My second uncle, also a brave warrior, was part of the iNgobamakhosi regiment. He was a ladies' man with three wives who, between them, had given him eight children. My father was the bravest and the wisest of the three. He was one of the most respected indunas in the land and had been appointed to join the prestigious inner circle of advisers to the king, spending most of his time with him at Ondini.

I missed my cousins. The Makhoba family was large and close and we did everything together, from sharing meals and thatching huts to working in the fields. My cousins and I spent a great deal of time making grass mats and plaiting each other's hair. I missed the times when we all went to the river to draw water – it was the best time of the day. We would undress and bathe in the river. We loved frolicking in the water, well aware that there were some young men lying in wait for us behind the bushes. We pretended we were not aware of their presence. The sound of our laughter reverberated as we dived in and out of the river naked. The older girls would tease the young men by openly flaunting their naked bums and breasts as they dipped into the water. When the men could no longer stand the girls' coquettish behaviour, they threatened us with abduction. Those of us who were still under age were envious of the games played by the older girls. We couldn't wait to grow up and qualify to participate in them.

Sitting idly in the cave, I often thought about the life I had left behind. I longed for the days when I looked after the goats, chasing after them in the open veld. I had my favourites who would test my patience by wandering deep into the woods, making the task of looking after them even more arduous. I had a great time with these creatures who are among the most agreeable animals under the sun. Unlike the cows that sometimes get into scuffles and pierce each other with their horns, goats have a gentle demeanour. All they need is to find fresh young succulent leaves to browse on and water to quench their thirst and they will happily gallop all over the place.

The mornings at our homestead were what I missed the most. This was a time of great activity as we got ready to milk the cows. The youngsters in charge of the calves were the first to rise and made sure that the calves were nowhere near the milking pen. Those of us tasked with the job of milking the cows would enter the kraal and fasten the heifers to be milked with leather strips over their heads and thongs to bind their hindlegs. The Makhoba family owned over sixty head of cattle. This number of cattle sharing one kraal made milking a time of jostling for position to do our work. Outside the kraal, the calves would hover around the entrance to the pen and bellow, demanding to suckle, while the heifers still waiting to be milked, paced about the kraal, itching to be relieved of the heavy weight in their udders. The cows that did not want to be milked made our task difficult. They kicked out with their bound hindlegs, sometimes hard enough to send both the can and the person milking flying.

As there was no boy in my family, my father decided to teach me how to milk. I was about eight years old when he first took me inside the kraal and showed me how to squat and hold the can firmly between my thighs and knees. At first I thought I would never get the hang of it. I remember the strange feeling I had the first time I touched the cows' udders, the sensation of handling the warm velvety skin of the teats made my skin crawl. But I soon became accustomed to the touch and began to enjoy pulling the warm hanging teats and to relish the soft sound made by the milk as it travelled from the udders to land in the can. There was competition among the Makhoba family milking troupe which serviced and provided the clan with milk. Even though I was a girl among boys, I made sure that I filled my can to the brim as everyone else did. But we had to make sure that we did not milk the cows dry. We had to leave some milk for the calves. The family was never short of milk. There was so much of it that we often offered the surplus to some of our widowed or orphaned neighbours.

Away from the rest of the family, I missed my grandmother the most. I longed for the moments when I went to her hut to share her evening meal of sour milk and ground sorghum. For some unexplained reason, her calabash seemed to produce the best sour milk in the homestead, thicker and creamier than anyone else's. I missed snuggling next to her on cold nights and sharing her warm blankets, which were made of skins that Father tanned from the hides of the animals he brought in from his hunting trips. He took great pride in working on the animal skins and turning them into blankets. He'd skin the animal and dry the hide for days. When dry, he applied herbs and fat to it and with his bare hands he kneaded the mixture into the hide until the leather was tanned and soft. He then took a smooth stone and painstakingly ironed over the leather and there it was – a blanket!

We were scared and unprotected, alone in the cave. It was no consolation that we were not the only ones whose able-bodied men were at war. Even boys too young to fight were tasked with the chores of carrying medicine, food and war essentials for the regiments.

Since my father was one of the king's most trusted advisers he spent a great deal of time at the palace at Ondini where King Cetshwayo held court with the elders, the scouts and the spies. There were also a few white people who served as advisers and interpreters to the king. Ondini was where the king met and entertained emissaries from foreign countries seeking to settle in Zululand and where he received European traders bringing him items such as knives and beads in exchange for land, cattle and ivory. Sometimes they brought large items such as beautifully carved chairs. The king also received European missionaries who were bent on converting the Zulu people to Christianity. Once King Cetshwayo questioned a missionary about the existence of God in relation to uMvelinqangi, the Creator whom the Zulu people worshipped and revered. The missionary told the king that the God he was introducing to the Zulu people was more powerful than all other gods. He described him as 'mkhulukhulu', *bigger than big*. The king shook his head and laughed and dismissed the missionary from his presence.

★

One night, as we were getting ready to sleep, we heard movement outside the cave. The sound of whatever was moving about was not a hoofed animal. We remained dead quiet. We heard the tree trunk covering the entrance to our abode move and the big stone that was the door shifted. The first thing that came to my mind was that the enemy had discovered our hideout and they were going to kill us. Mother must have thought the same thing for with the speed of lightning she went for her spear and waited for the intruder. The blade tore at the darkness, glistening, as she lifted it in readiness to strike whoever was entering our sanctuary. My sister and I seized our assegais in preparation to strike the intruder or intruders. We had often practised this drill as we expected to be attacked at any time. We did not know whether it was the enemy or perhaps one of our people who had been captured by the enemy and was now being used to spy. We were ready to strike whoever ventured into our sanctuary. We had the advantage because we knew the layout of the cave and we were accustomed to the darkness. Besides, the cave could only be accessed by one person at a time, so we were ready to receive whoever came in.

Evidently realising that we were ready to strike, we heard a voice: 'Hhayi bo, it's me, your father.'

Although we hadn't seen Father for many days, we immediately recognised his voice and put our weapons away. I was so happy to see him I wanted to rush to him but was constrained by the size of the cave. I had to be patient and wait for him to crawl to where we were sitting.

He was carrying his spear, a shield, an assegai and a rifle with a bayonet. He put these down and sat next to Mother. He looked tired. Although I was thrilled to have him with us, I was more interested in the rifle. I had heard so much about this weapon but I had never seen one before that night. I had been told that a mere touch could kill many people. I couldn't take my eyes off it nor could I resist the temptation to touch it. I extended my hand with the intention of doing so but Father must have read my mind because he got hold of my hand just when I was about to touch it.

'Don't touch that,' he said. 'It's not a toy.'

Embarrassed at being chided by my dad, I flinched and moved closer to the little space next to my sister, away from my parents. Father realised that I was upset and proffered his hand. I took it and he pulled me towards his chest and stroked my head and said: 'I don't want you to touch this weapon until I have taught you how to use it. It is powerful and dangerous. I promise you, I will teach you when the war over.'

I knew it would be a long time before that happened. It was obvious that the hostilities were not about to stop. He enquired about our welfare. I told him that living in the cave was intolerable and that I was missing the rest of the family. He said I should persevere, promising me that it would not be long before our lives became normal again. He said he also missed us.

Lately, Father had been concerned about the king and what was happening to the nation. King Cetshwayo faced enormous problems. The nation was under siege. The war between the Zulus and the foreigners had started in mid-summer and we were now in the middle of winter and there was as yet no sign of the hostilities abating. The king had confessed to Father that the events in the country had forced him to recall the prophetic words uttered by his uncle King Shaka who, as he took his last breath, had said to his assassins, his brothers Dingane and Mhlangana: 'You think by killing me you will rule this land? I can see the birds hovering over the horizon, they will be the rulers.'

Father was echoing the words of some of the old people with whom we had shared the first cave. I remembered how the veterans spoke of the anguish and suffering the nation experienced. The king had lost thousands of warriors and cattle. Many homesteads had been burnt down and abandoned and the landscape was dotted with white settlements. Initially the nation had welcomed King Dingane's ascendance to the throne because they thought he would put an end to the reign of terror which they had experienced during King Shaka's time. They saw King Dingane as the liberator who would bring back the good old days

43

of living in peace and harmony. It didn't take long for that bubble to burst. Shortly after coming to power Dingane stirred the hornets' nest by killing a Boer delegation under the leadership of Piet Retief, who had gone to him to negotiate for land to settle on. By killing Retief and his followers, Dingane had plunged the nation into a bloody confrontation with the Boers who were fleeing from British rule in the Cape Colony and hoping to settle in Zululand.

With the words of Shaka ringing in his ears, Dingane thought that by murdering the sixty-nine Boer commandos and their leader he would stem the tide of invasion. Instead, the massacre of the Boers by the Zulu warriors was to unleash a sequence of vicious events, the devastating outcome of which changed the history of the region for ever. The protracted battles between the Zulus and the Boers continued until the Zulus were vanquished and divided. Some sought refuge with white settlers in Natal. Dingane fled from his land and was later assassinated in Ngwavuma. His half-brother Mpande succeeded him.

Mpande, the ambiguous Zulu king, was regarded by many of his subjects as a lame duck. He was the first Zulu king to be installed by foreigners, something which was offensive to the Zulu people. As a prince from a pedigree of brave warriors, Mpande had not carved a name for himself as a warrior. While some of the problems he encountered were of his own making, he inherited many from his brother Dingane. Mpande's rule was marred by controversy. He was seen by many old Zulu people as a white man's lackey. Zulu sovereignty had been eroded and foreigners were dictating to the Zulu monarch. There was a scramble for land and Zulu people were now competing with strangers for their land. Cattle thieving between the two groups became the order of the day.

White historians and writers often described King Mpande as intelligent and shrewd, as the one Zulu king who understood politics. They tended to ignore the role played by King Cetshwayo who tried everything in his power to protect the Zulu nation but failed dismally at trying to keep the white invaders at bay. King Cetshwayo had succeeded his father after a protracted battle for power between him and his half-brother Mbuyazi who was killed at the battle of Ndondakusuka. From the moment King Cetshwayo ascended the throne he was faced with the problem of invasion. Every day he learned that the whites were not only in Natal but that new settlements had encroached on his side of the land. He knew that he had a responsibility to protect his people from the invaders. Failure to do so would bring about the realisation of Shaka's prophecy, that Zululand would be ruled by the birds. Cetshwayo was wise and had the interests of his people at heart. Yet he didn't understand the mentality of his adversaries, nor could he speak their language. He was at the mercy of the interpreters, who were white.

My father and I were in the habit of discussing many things. Before the war broke out, he had often come back from Ondini in a depressed state of mind. He spent hours talking to Mother about the state of the nation and how the country was in trouble, that white people wanted to rob us of our land. I was curious about these people whom I had never seen. From the description given by those who had seen them, they seemed like monsters. I asked my father to take me to where the white people were. He shook his head and said: 'You don't want to see those people. You must pray that you never ever get to see them for as long as you live.' That aroused my curiosity even more. I would have paid any price to get to see the strange white people.

'You, my girl, are my boy,' Father said to me. 'You are clever and brave. I know you will be a fighter. That is why I named you Nombhosho, a bullet. You will come out of any situation unscathed. You are a warrior.'

Father raised me as a boy and he taught me many things. Few girls could undertake some of the tasks which I was able to perform. I could milk a cow at the age of eight; administer medicine to sick cattle; I could repair damaged houses. My father and I would sometimes go hunting. We spent days away from home stalking wild animals. If we were lucky and killed an animal, we would, with the hounds barking in glee, walk back home carrying the carcass suspended on a pole between us. Everybody would be happy to have us back because they knew they would be treated to a feast. I assisted Father with the skinning of the animal. He also taught me how to fight with sticks. That night in the cave we chatted for some time before he could pay attention to my little sister. Mother told him that there was no food in the cave. We survived mainly on roots and rats, wild fruit and dry ground sorghum, umcaba.

This visit was no different from the others. Every time Father came he would talk about the war, its progress, or the lack of it. As the king's adviser, he was part of the delegation that met Somtseu, Theophilus Shepstone. King Cetshwayo's delegation usually included John Dunn, known as Jantoni by the Zulus. Jantoni had grown up among the Zulu people, spoke impeccable Zulu and led a polygamous lifestyle. He had one white wife and several Zulu wives and many white and coloured children. He was a frequent visitor to the palace where he served as both translator and adviser to the king. AmaZulu disliked and mistrusted Jantoni but the king seemed to like him and he was often part of the king's delegation to Somtseu. But when the war between the English and the

Zulus broke out, Jantoni's true colours emerged, proving that the Ama-Zulu's suspicions about him had not been misplaced. Jantoni denounced his Zulu ties and fought on the side of the English.

However, the Zulu people hated Somtseu the most. They perceived him as someone who wanted to impoverish the nation by making preposterous demands on the king, someone who wanted to take over as king. The third villain was Lord Chelmsford.

Father openly disliked Somtseu, Jantoni and, to a lesser degree, Lord Chelmsford. He had some respect for Lord Chelmsford, arguing that unlike Somtseu who issued ultimatums from the safe distance and offices of Pietermaritzburg, Lord Chelmsford was a soldier who was in the trenches with his men. Being a warrior himself, Father respected that about Chelmsford.

*

Many years ago in the 1970s, before I knew about my family history at Isandlwana, I accompanied a group of English tourists to the area. We arrived late in the afternoon and could not secure a tour guide. As we were wondering what we should do, we were accosted by a small boy of about twelve years. He seemed knowledgeable about the area and he took us around, even as far as Rorke's Drift. At the end of the tour we gave him some money and asked him his name. 'Chelmsford' was his name, he told us. As he showed us around the battlefields, he had pointed to a spot and told us that that was where the Chelmsford, after whom he had been named, had sat and eaten his breakfast.

I have often pondered the reason for parents naming their son Chelmsford and thought it strange even though I know that Africans often name their children according to family or national events, or the place of their birth – my own name NomaVenda, is a reminder to my parents of the time they spent in Venda. For instance, I know a few people in Zululand who, when the National Party withdrew from the Commonwealth and dropped the British pound and introduced rands and cents, named children born in those years Malentsha, new money. Recently I came across a few youngsters in Moroka around the Regina Mundi Cathedral who were born in 1994. They were named Democracy.

★

Once Father had finished talking to us, it was time to go to sleep. I prepared our grass mats and motioned my sister to join me. But I was far from falling asleep. I was curious about the purpose of Father's visit. Of course he had come to check on us but I knew that he must be troubled by something and he had come to unburden to his wife.

My dad trusted my mother's counsel. She was a wise woman who listened and could put matters into perspective. Her intelligence was probably shaped by her father Umthokonjo ka Ntshangase who had been part of Shaka's amaKwenkwe regiment and was later promoted to be one of Shaka's indunas and advisers. Like my father, my grandfather Umthokonjo spent most of his time at KwaDukuza, King Shaka's palace. Perhaps that was why mother was tolerant of our dad's long spells of absence from home.

From where I was sleeping, I could see and hear my parents talking. My mother sat with her legs stretched out on the grass mat next to Dad whose eyes were fixed on the ground.

'Tell me, Nombhosho's dad, what is troubling you so?' Mother asked.

'So much is wrong, my wife. I do not know where to begin. Yesterday, the enemy cornered us and Mbilini was killed. I don't know what is going to happen when those scavengers reach Ulundi. They will kill everyone and take everything.'

Mbilini was one of Cetshwayo's most trusted warriors. He was a Swazi national who had defected to Zululand where he had made a name for himself as a brave and outstanding fighter. Ordinary-looking, Mbilini was tall and lean with an unimposing personality. A stranger would never guess that he was a fearless warrior hated by notable people like Somtseu who was aware of the many skirmishes Mbilini had been involved in. His countenance often demanded a second look, because he was a simple man who did not care to wear the colourful apparel of beads and feathers favoured by some of the more flamboyant warriors. He was most unassuming about his looks. If anyone dared to compliment him on his fighting prowess he would burst out laughing in his tenor voice. Members of his regiment referred to him as 'Ibhubesi eliphansi', the gentle lion. He was utterly loyal to Cetshwayo, ready to lay down his life to help the Zulus to destroy the English army. He had vowed not to rest until the enemy had been vanquished and to ensure that those who remained had been sent back to the sea from whence they had come.

Mbilini had led about five thousand assegai-wielding men to face the rifle-armed British army along the uKhahlamba escarpment on a wintry morning in July. The battle had lasted about five hours with the Zulu men stubbornly fighting on, seemingly oblivious of the bullets raining down on them. The Zulus had planned their attack carefully with the assistance of the scouts who had been watching the manoeuvres of the enemy for days.

The scouts had observed the wagons arriving and the tents being pitched. They saw some of the Zulus who had defected and who now served the white army as servants ferrying boxes into the tents. Some were carting water from the river to the tents. It was a warm winter's day and some of the soldiers were loitering about cleaning their guns; others were writing letters to their loved ones while their Zulu servants toiled. King Cetshwayo's regiments hid behind the mountain and waited until it was dark. They were in high spirits and could smell victory. Their scouts had described the area accurately. It was clear to the Zulu regiment lying in wait that the white people were oblivious of the danger lurking behind the mountain.

Meanwhile the English had reconnoitred the area and were satisfied that their plan to attack the Zulus in a few days' time would be successful. This time they were going to drive the Zulus further away from the fertile lands and the Natal border. The areas around the Tugela basin had already been seized. What was left to achieve was for the Zulus to be moved further into the interior, into the barren parts of the country.

Mbilini's men had expected their attack to be a walkover. They had conducted a thorough reconnaissance and were of the opinion that they had the advantage. They were going to pounce on the enemy at its weakest moment, when they were still in bed. They attacked the English camp in the small hours of the morning when the unsuspecting soldiers were deep in slumber in their tents and wagons. The Zulu warriors anticipated catching the invaders literally with their pants down, knowing it would take time for them to get dressed and get their sophisticated weaponry ready for battle. They knew they would first have to get rid of the deserters – those Zulus who had defected and were guarding the camp. Once they were out of the way, they would unleash their spears on the English soldiers.

What the Zulu regiment did not know was that the Zulu servants guarding the site had been trained in the handling of the bayonets in the case of such an eventuality. They did not know that some of the deserters were now part of the English army. Instead of the Zulus launching a surprise attack on unsuspecting soldiers, they were met by their own people who fought exceedingly competently. By the time the English soldiers woke up, the servants and the Zulu soldiers had triumphantly held the fort. It did not take long for the English soldiers to affix their bayonets and put gunpowder into the cannons to fire at the charging Zulu men. As the sun rose, it became clear to the Zulus that they were losing the battle and had to retreat. By noon, thousands of Zulu men lay dead. Amongst them was Mbilini.

The distressing news of Mbilini's death was a heavy blow to King Cetshwayo, as well as to my father. Not only did Mbilini die at the height of the war, he died at a time when it was becoming obvious to the Zulus that they were losing the war.

Mbilini's death coincided with the defection of Hhamu, the king's half-brother, to the British. The king felt Hhamu's betrayal intensely. He took with him an entire regiment, weakening the Zulu nation both physically and spiritually. It was no secret that these men would now be used by the English against the Zulus. With the death of Mbilini, the king had told Father that he felt as though the earth was shifting underneath him.

'I know the king will never surrender to the white man,' I heard my father tell my mother. 'He has told me on numerous occasions that he would die before he let the invaders grab the land of Mthaniya. You know what saddens me the most? It is to watch the king suffer day in and day out with reports of how his people have been slaughtered by the invaders. Every time a report of that nature reaches his ears he dies a little. It's so painful to see how he is tormented. You'd be surprised to see how much he has aged since the war broke out.'

'The king has to be careful,' Mother said. 'You remember Shaka's prophecy to Dingane and Mhlangana: "You think by killing me you will rule this land. I can see the birds hovering above. They will rule this land." We have sacrificed too much to give in now.'

I watched and listened to my parents talk until I fell asleep. When I woke up the next morning, my father had gone.

PART TWO

The Search

*I*n 2010, Sis Ahh's children threw a huge eightieth birthday party for her. My brothers and sisters and our offspring converged on Hlabisa to be part of the celebrations. The event kicked off at noon with a mass at the Anglican Church next to the hospital, and later moved to the Luthuli homestead, Sis Ahh's home, where a cow had been slaughtered to feed the guests who had come from many parts of South Africa.

In the evening, when most of the visitors had left and only we, her sisters and our children and some of her closest relatives remained, we were housed in one of her spare bedrooms – a huge room that accommodates four double beds and a single bed. We dubbed it 'the Holiday Inn'. The room was en suite, boasting a large bath, a shower and a toilet. What an improvement we commented, recalling that during apartheid days rural areas were without electricity and running water. Those were the days when a visit to these parts of the country meant that for the duration of one's stay one had to undergo the ghastly experience of using pit toilets. I still remember the frustration I suffered when visiting our parents' home and had to use a pit latrine. I was petrified since I had been reliably informed by the locals that snakes, particularly in summer, often sought shade inside the toilets. So I never set foot inside a pit toilet. Instead, whenever I felt the need to empty my bowels I would ask my husband to drive me to the hospital where Sis Ahh worked. This meant travelling a distance of about nine kilometres. And as matters of the bowels go, by the time we arrived at the hospital, the urge to use the toilet would be gone.

Now there we were, young and old females sharing this huge bedroom. We were like high school girls having a pyjama party. No man was allowed in the room except for Sibali, our brother-in-law who is married to our cousin Ndethi. Sibali is extremely possessive of his wife and cannot countenance being without her. He was making a nuisance of himself by frequently knocking on our door, claiming he could not find his toothbrush or some other minor item. Each time he came around, we would all of us simultaneously shout at him to leave the room. But that did not deter him. He would be back again, until ultimately we told Ndethi to vacate the room and join the men who were enjoying themselves further down the passage drinking all types of liquor.

Sisters, mothers and daughters and cousins frolicked in this room like little girls. Those of us who were older regaled the younger ones with stories about our youth. The stories that the group was more interested in were the ones about Sis Ahh. My other sister Sis B – Beatrice – is five years younger than Sis Ahh and she too had many stories to tell.

One of the anecdotes that had us in stitches was how Sis Ahh used to fall asleep in church while playing the cornet. As children of a Salvation Army officer, our father taught all of us, girls and boys alike, to play a musical instrument. There were nine of us and father often boasted that the church doors would always be open whether the congregants came to church or not as he had his own Khumalo band.

'We would be in the middle of a hymn and Sis Ahh, who was playing the cornet – what you guys refer to as a trumpet – would fall asleep,' Sis B related. 'As soon as we heard the music score drop to the floor we would know that Sisi was asleep which meant the band would be without the lead instrument. Father would come down from the pulpit and smack her on the head, not too hard, but enough to wake her up. He was gentle with her because she was his first-born child.'

'You guys have no idea how much trouble I've courted with my sleeping habits,' said Sis Ahh, laughing at herself. 'I once came back from night duty dog tired. I had a small baby then, I think it was Khosi and she must have been about four months old. I quickly had a bath and went to bed. While I was sleeping, the nanny brought the baby to me to suckle. Half awake, I took the child and thrust my teat into its tiny mouth and collapsed into a slumber. I was woken up by Mshibe (her husband's clan name) who must have been alerted that something was not right by the sounds the child was making as it struggled for breath under my udders. I had never seen him so angry with me. He pushed me away from the baby, removed the blanket and gave me a solid spanking on my bum, screaming: "What are you doing, MaKhumalo, you want to kill my child with your big mammaries!"'

My sister was well endowed in that department. We all laughed even though we couldn't imagine Madlanduna as we often called him − another name for the Luthuli clan − hurting a fly. He was the gentlest person I knew. He not only loved his wife, he also cherished members of his wife's family.

The night progressed. Gradually we moved away from telling jokes about Sis Ahh to remembering our departed relatives. Obviously the first victim of our humour was our mother − Sister J. After we had exhausted stories about her, we moved on to talking about our uncles, particularly Qholwayo, Gogo's first-born son. He was the spitting image of the Kenyan president Jomo Kenyatta. The resemblance was so pronounced it could have been used as evidence that proved some anthropologists' theory that the Zulu people originally came from the Kenyan savannahs and drifted down Africa to settle on the sloping green valleys of Zululand. Uncle Qholwayo was dark skinned with a round face and large broad nose, topped with a manageable salt and pepper Afro similar to Kenyatta's. What a colourful person he was! He was born to entertain crowds. And could he sing!

Once, when he was released from a short spell of prison detention on trumped-up charges, he composed a song whose lyrics were 'wakhal'eboshiwe, kwaNongoma' – the one who wept while incarcerated at Nongoma prison. He sang this ditty with such passion that only a heartless listener could miss the pain he had suffered in jail. From that time onwards his name became Makhaleboshiwe or Makhala for short.

Sis Ahh recalled stories of another uncle, Uyikhwama, a man-about-town who spent most of his life in Johannesburg's gambling dens. He'd often go home penniless.

'When Gogo chastised him for not giving her money he would say: "Tell me, how many pints of your milk did I suckle so that I must pay you back?"'

We heard many stories that night but at some point my niece Xoli, whom I had informed of my endeavours in writing a book about okaMakhoba, thought it would be appropriate to hear stories about Gogo from the horse's mouth.

'Mamkhulu, tell us about okaMakhoba,' said Xoli. 'She is such an inspiration to us. How I wish I could have met her.'

'When are you guys going to stop asking me about things that happened many years ago?' said Sis Ahh. 'Besides, I'm not the only one who knows about Gogo. Why don't you ask your uncles about her? Or our cousins Thende, Mbuzeli and Mangondo. All those people lived with okaMakhoba, you must talk to them.'

Realising that we were not relenting in our quest to know about Gogo, she then said: 'Where do I begin? You know the story of how the English invaded Zululand and drove away the local people, sending them to the mountains. What more do you want to know?'

'We want to know how life was for our ancestors, how they endured the hardships,' said Xoli. 'We particularly want to know the role played by our great-grandmother okaMakhoba.' Xoli is a producer at one of the country's leading

television stations. I could tell that she was already figuring out how she was going to structure a documentary about Gogo.

Sis Ahh responded. 'Gogo, together with her mother and little sister, lived in the caves in the Shiyane mountains, surviving on roots and rats. Occasionally, their father Makhoba – our great-grandfather – would travel from the king's palace at Ondini to the mountains, a journey which took him days because there were no buses transporting people in those days. He did this trip, which is about fifty kilometres, barefooted. And since his country was at war, he had to be vigilant and watch out for the English soldiers, because they would kill him on sight or abduct him and turn him into a slave.

'Gogo described their abode in the mountain as a single entrance cave that was secured by a huge boulder against which was an enormous tree trunk. A small strip was left open to let in light and a bit of air. The interior was perpetually damp and since the cave was a narrow structure, there was little room to manoeuvre. They could only lie down or sit with their legs folded. The ground was covered with grass, soft tree leaves and branches which served as a mattress beneath their grass mats. To gain entry to the cave one had to crawl, one person at a time. Apart from the chirping birds in the morning that heralded the beginning of another day, there was no way of telling night from day.'

The mood in the room had changed from jovial to serious as we listened to Sis Ahh, who at that point had transformed to personify Gogo for the benefit of her narration.

★

On this occasion, Father came during the day. As soon as he entered the cave, he said to Mother: 'Come, mfazi, woman. I'm moving you out of here. The invaders claim we have killed a prince from over the seas and they are out for revenge. You are too close to the enemy. You have to leave this place.'

Mother clapped her hands in disbelief. 'Aren't all these invaders from over the seas? And what was this prince doing in our land?' she asked. 'It serves him right to die because he came here to kill us.'

'Don't argue with me, mfazi. I don't know where these people are from. The king has been told that Somtseu is hopping mad because we killed someone who is very important. I don't know who he was. All I know is that I have to move you from here. Come, get ready. Let's go.'

We were to learn years later that the white man who had been killed in battle was the Imperial French Prince Louis Napoleon who was visiting South Africa to witness the war between the Zulus and the English. The war was big news in Europe.

There was nothing to pack since we had been reduced to being vagrants in the land of our forefathers, living off rats and roots. Our possessions amounted to empty calabashes and grass mats. When I came out of the cave the sun hit me hard. I could not see a thing.

'Baba, I cannot see. Ma, I am blind!' I cried.

Father picked me up and put me on his shoulders. He assured me that my sight would soon be restored.

'You have been cooped up in that dungeon for too long. Your eyes will soon get used to the sun,' said Father. He was right. Within a few minutes I was able to see again.

This time Father was not alone. He was accompanied by about fifty warriors who were armed to the teeth. Within the group were some boys carrying fighting gear such as assegais, spears and rifles. There were also boys carrying chunks of beef and corn. Some of the meat was cooked. The sight of food made me salivate. We had not eaten proper food in a long while. But aside from drooling over the meat, I was so happy to see my father even though he seemed agitated. He told us that the white people were wreaking havoc in the region, killing and pillaging anything and everything they came into contact with. Villages had been burnt down, women and children were fleeing.

With my sister Ndumbutshu on Mother's back and me on Dad's shoulders, we began the long walk to the other side of the mountain, accompanied by the young warriors who were in high spirits. Some of the men were chanting war songs to the accompaniment of umakhweyana and isituruturu, the traditional Zulu musical instruments. Others were prancing about and engaging in mock stick fights. Apart from my father and some of the older members of the regiment who were obviously concerned about the turn of events, the mood around us was buoyant. A stranger would not have guessed that we were being hounded like animals and that the pursuing hounds were only a few miles away. Ahead of them Zulu scouts were reconnoitring.

We walked the entire day passing villages whose inhabitants had fled leaving their homes in ruins. In some places it was obvious that the owners must have left in a hurry because when we entered the huts looking for water and something to eat we found items such as calabashes and cooking utensils made out of clay – such as udiwo and imbhenge – still intact. We stumbled over bones of animals that must have been dogs, left behind by their owners as they ran for cover. They had obviously died of starvation. The empty kraals next to the homesteads echoed the story of utter desolation.

In the afternoon we came to a river. The sight of water and birds tweeting in the trees was wonderful. It was like being at home. Without wasting any time, the young warriors and I jumped into the water and bathed before refilling the calabashes. The feeling of water on my body after weeks of not washing was a thrill beyond compare. Even though it was the height of winter, the water was warm and inviting. We swam and washed and played in the river until Father became annoyed and told us to get out, reminding us that we still had a long distance to travel.

After we emerged from the water some of the warriors and I joined the older men who were having a meal of meat roasted on an open fire. This was accompanied by mealie cobs which the warriors had taken from the fields left by villagers fleeing from the war. We washed the food down with fresh water from the river and for a moment forgot that we were the white men's prey.

After the sumptuous meal we were on the road again. Accompanied by the young warriors, we climbed up and down many cliffs until we reached a part of the mountain shaped like a basin. On entering the hollow we found a long passage which led to what looked like a hut. It was obvious that the place had at some point been somebody's home and refuge. We found broken pieces of calabash and a grinding stone. The men helped to clear the place and collected some branches and leaves to make the shelter habitable. When they left, they gave us a large chunk of meat and some roasted corn.

The warriors took off in high spirits, once again singing war songs. They were going after the enemy who had pitched their tents on the plateau on the other side of the mountain. They anticipated meeting up with the other regiments who had headed off earlier on.

My father spent the night with us before leaving for Ondini in the early hours of the morning to hold counsel with the king. Once more we were left on our own. We didn't know what to expect. We were now established cave dwellers, vagrants, dispossessed folk. Through the experience of living in caves we had become acclimatised to living in darkness. We were lonely and often brooded about the whereabouts of our extended family. We didn't know where they were or if they were still alive. We felt cut off from the world. I remember those days as the darkest time of my life.

During our time on the mountain, we were never spared the chilling sound of gunfire. Night after night we would lie awake listening to the muffled B-O-O-M. This echo would cut through the eerie peace in the cave, leaving us shaking with fear and thinking the end had come. Sometimes the intervals between the stillness and the sound of shooting lasted long enough for us to think that the fighting was over, only for it to strike again: B-O-O-O-M.

In the beginning the sound of guns going off was a cold reminder that we were living on the precipice of death. Shaking like wet puppies, we held tightly on to our mother who stoically sat up with her legs stretched out in front of her, staring into space as though daring death to come. We had been told that the invaders' weapons could sniff out people hiding in caves and kill them. We had every reason to believe those stories because in our flight from the Redcoats we had come across many corpses, victims of the powerful guns.

One particular night had been no different from the many other nights of gunshots in the hours of darkness. The shooting stopped around midnight. Only then were we able to catch a nap with the expectation of waking up to another empty and lonely day. But we were woken early by a searing lament coming from the foot of the mountain. The unmistakable echo of pain pierced into the cave at a time when we could have been sleeping.

'Uphelile uZulu! Sizokwenzenjani? Uphelile uZulu.' The Zulu nation is finished. What are we going to do? the women wailed.

At first I thought I was dreaming but as the wailing continued, I knew that I was not. I opened my eyes to find Mother sitting upright on the grass mat. I looked at her. Even in the darkness that enveloped us in the cave, I could see the fear in her eyes. Like me, she was petrified.

Suddenly she said: 'I'm not going to die in here without knowing what is happening outside. We've got to get out of here.' She grabbed Ndumbutshu and ran out of the cave. I followed her.

The sun was just coming up as we ran towards the edge of the mountain. We looked down. From where we stood, we could clearly hear and see what was happening at the foot of the mountain. A group of women, a crowd of about sixty, most of them carrying babies on their backs, others with bundles on their heads, was walking past the mountain. They were howling, a lament that seemed to emanate from somewhere deep in their bellies. Some wept with their arms and hands folded over their heads. They moved as though they were in a trance, propelled only by their pain to keep on walking.

One of the older women who appeared to be their leader kept urging them on. 'Come on, move. There is no time to waste feeling sorry for yourselves. We have to get away and find a place where we can protect our children. They are the future of uZulu. Come on, move.'

The wailing women continued walking. They were all skinny, malnourished. Many were almost too weak to walk. Others tripped and fell as they walked, but amidst the tears, pain and fatigue, they rose from the ground and walked on. There was no one to console them. There was no one to say a soothing word to the distraught women engulfed in the pain of their loss. They went on, carrying their burdens. The heart-rending lament was something I had never heard before. Even though I was a child, their anguish struck at the very core of my existence and I felt my stomach twisting into knots. Quietly I asked, 'Senzeni? What have we done to deserve this?'

Mother called to the women: 'Yini? Kwenzenjani?' What is happening? she asked.

The wind carried her voice in the opposite direction from the women. They did not hear her calling to them, nor did they realise that there was somebody on the top of the mountain. They just carried on their journey to who-knows-where. I stood next to my mother, confused and wondering what was going on at the bottom of the mountain.

The women drifted further and further away from us and were soon out of sight, but their wailing could be heard for a long time. Mother slowly picked her way back to the cave. My little sister and I followed her. But before we entered the cave my eyes fell on a package placed neatly under a stone a few feet away from the entrance to the cave. I moved towards it and took a closer look. It was a bag made out of goatskin.

I knew the pouch like the back of my hand. And I knew immediately what it contained. My father's weapons. I had handled that pouch on numerous occasions and had no doubt what it was. But I couldn't understand why it was lying there. Father had taken his weapons with him when he went to Mahlabathini. I had never seen him without his spear and assegai. Their presence was perplexing. On the other hand, what was not perplexing in those days? We were nomads living in caves. We were hunted and killed like wild animals. What was perplexing about finding my father's weapons under a stone? What was astonishing was the fact that we were still alive.

The more I looked at the package under the stone, the more worried I became. The presence of the arms at this spot made my heart beat faster. I suddenly knew with a terrible certainty that something bad had happened. Maybe it was the effect of the women's lament that had unsettled me. I looked at the weapons and tried hard to justify their presence under the stone. The only explanation I could think of was that perhaps Father had been around the cave sometime during the night. Surely, if that had been the case, he would have come in to see us. Why would he leave his arms outside unattended? It was so unlike him because he was meticulous about his weapons.

I lost interest in the plight of the women below the mountain as I now had a puzzle to solve. I looked at my mother who was about to enter the cave. It was obvious to me that she had not seen the package of arms. I knew that if she had she would have picked them up. I moved closer to her and took her arm thus stopping her from entering the cave. She paused and looked at me with enquiring eyes. I nudged her with my right elbow and with my left hand I pointed at the package. She looked where I was pointing. She saw the pouch. She picked it up, emptied out its contents and inspected the weapons thoroughly.

Next thing she emitted one piercing scream and dropped down on the hard ground. I looked at her and waited for her to get up. She didn't. She appeared to be asleep. I found that odd. I could not understand why she was sleeping on the ground. Surely, if she felt drowsy, she would have gone back to the cave and slept on the grass mat. I waited for her to wake up but she didn't. I became worried. I knelt next to her and asked her gently to wake up. Nothing happened. Then I panicked. In between sobs I shook her frantically shouting, 'Mother, Mother, wake up!'

She remained still on the ground and I feared the worst. I had a weird feeling that she had died. I had seen many corpses in the course of our journey, but I had never seen anybody die before my eyes. I was confronted with a situation that I knew nothing about. I continued shaking her, imploring her to wake up but she didn't respond.

My little sister Ndumbutshu was going berserk, crying and stamping her feet and screaming, 'Ma–ma, Ma–ma.' A voice inside me said 'pour water on her'. I ran inside the cave and brought out the calabash containing our last bit of water. I sprinkled it over her. She lay quietly for quite a long time. Although I thought she was dead I did not give up. I continued shaking her, trying to get her to wake up.

Eventually she came to. She sat up but seemed in a daze as her eyes roamed around her. I think she must have remembered what had caused her to faint. Without warning, she began crying. She cried, and cried, and cried. She was inconsolable. Crying is infectious. Soon we were all crying. There we were, on the crest of the mountain, on our knees and sobbing.

We were oblivious to the danger we faced. Where we were, we were easy targets for the enemy and for wild animals. We were all alone with no one to comfort or protect us. It was as though the entire world was swallowing us up. We were on the highest peak of that part of the earth, far from the valleys where the battles were being fought, yet we were vulnerable. The situation was made even more frightening because my sister and I didn't know why Mother was crying. In the many months we had been on the mountain we had faced many kinds of danger and not once had she shed a tear. I thought whatever had brought about her anguish must be life threatening.

We cried for as long as Mother did. When she had exhausted her tears, she put the arms back into the pouch and said: 'My children, your father is no more. He has died in battle. As you can see, these are his weapons. They have been brought to us to inform us of his death.'

She obviously did not know who had brought the arms but she knew that Zulu custom dictates that where possible the fallen warrior's arms must be returned to his family.

It was now my turn to go crazy. To be told that my father had died was the last thing I had expected to hear. How could my father die? He was invincible. He was the strongest and bravest man I had ever known. Who would dare stand in front of him and cause him harm? Nobody could kill my father. Had I not seen him many times stalking wild animals and killing them with his assegai? Was he not the bravest warrior in all of Zululand? My father was not dead!

I was not only sobbing, I was yelling at the top of my voice. Mother held me tight and begged me to be quiet, pleading with me to accept what had happened. I tried in vain to wrench free from her clutches but she held me tight. I wanted to run away to a place where nobody would find me. I could not face the reality of not ever seeing my father again. Mother held me until all my energy had dissipated.

Once I stopped crying, I collected my thoughts and reality stepped in. I thought there was something mysterious about the arms 'story'. As far as we knew, Father was no longer attached to any regiment. He had, in spite of his fighting prowess, been relieved of battle duties and promoted to being the king's full-time adviser. How could he be dead? If he was dead, it could only mean he had been at the battle front. When and why had he been redeployed? What did the king have to say about this? If Father was dead, where was the king? These questions flooded into my mind. Could it be that was what the women had been wailing about? That Father and the king were dead?

At this point, Mother had sobered up and had her strength back. Without warning, she told us we were vacating the cave. 'We can no longer stay here. We have to find people to tell us what is going on,' she said.

'Could it be that the women were crying because Father and the king are dead?' I asked my mother. 'You heard them say uZulu was finished. The king is uZulu; what do you think?'

'Child, I do not have the answers to your questions. For now, I want us to leave this place.'

I asked her if we were going back home. She merely shook her head and said, 'Let's go.'

She carried my sister on her back and I took my father's weapons and our grass mats and we started our descent from the mountain. The sun was now high in the sky and we were panting and sweating. My body could hardly carry me. I was weak from hunger and from crying. I longed to slumber under the trees but that was a luxury I could ill afford. We had to leave the mountain.

It took us half the day to get to the foot of the mountain. We were tired, thirsty and hungry as we picked our way carefully around the bushes before the clearing leading to the valley. We had to watch out for wild animals, as well as for the Redcoats. There was the added danger of being abducted by the Zulu people who had capitulated to the foreigners. Some of them were used by their masters to hunt for able-bodied Zulus to work as slaves for white people or to be part of the white army, although they were not given guns.

Slowly and painstakingly, we made our way out of the bushes and into the clearing. We arrived at what seemed like a well-travelled road. It was early afternoon and the sun was at its worst. There was not a cloud in the sky and the hot air seemed to carry an unrecognisable stench. We continued walking in the hope that we would come across a river but instead the road took us to the most unforgettable sight we would ever witness.

On our journey we had experienced many heart-rending sights but nothing could have prepared us for what we found in the valley below the mountain. In the past months we had come across many corpses, bodies of people who had either died from wounds inflicted in battle or who had died of hunger. We had seen skeletons lying in the veld. I thought I had witnessed enough pain and suffering to last me a lifetime. I was wrong. I also thought I had become immune to pain. Again, I was wrong.

This place had obviously been a battlefield. It seemed as though the entire valley was covered with corpses, mostly Zulus but also a few white soldiers in their white helmets and red jackets. Semi-clad Zulu warriors lay next to their spears. There were so many of them it was as though somebody had deliberately scattered the bodies all over the place. Feathers, beads, shields and assegais were strewn everywhere. The dead warriors' blood was drying and flies were buzzing on the gaping wounds while vultures were also at work, tearing the flesh off the corpses. The heat of the sun was relentless and the stench from the dead bodies was unbearable.

As we stood there trying to make sense of the scene before us, we spotted a wagon approaching the area. Fearing that it could be the enemy, we hid behind the nearby bushes. We sat quietly and watched it pull up next to the battlefield. Some Zulu people disembarked. They were wearing white people's clothes and spoke in hushed tones. They seemed to be in some sort of hurry to get away. I would later learn that they were Zulu people who had deserted the king and had chosen to go and work for the invaders. They began loading the white corpses on to the wagon. They also collected the weapons and war paraphernalia belonging to the whites. When they had completed their task, they rode off, leaving behind the bodies of the Zulu warriors to their fate among vultures and wild animals.

I could not understand how human beings could be so discriminatory. Why not at least dig shallow graves to bury their own kind and then cart off the invaders to their prestigious burial grounds? Would that have been too much to ask? Little did I know that in time I would see even more unpalatable and unacceptable behaviour directed at our people by the deserters.

We remained in hiding until the men with the horse wagon were out of sight.

We were thirsty and hungry. Mother said we should take our minds off food, so as not to feel the hunger pangs. We crossed many rivers but they were dry. We tried to dig in the earth for roots, particularly in the

EYES IN THE NIGHT

ground that was once river banks. We managed to find a few unpalatable roots but we were not sure if they were safe for us to eat. Yet we had no option but to chew on the bitter-tasting plants. We slept during the day and walked at night. Most days we slept in tree tops to be out of the reach of wild animals.

On the third day of aimless walking, we came across a group of people, mostly women and children, who had put up a camp site next to a ravine. The site was not only well hidden but it was impenetrable. The three of us stood for a long time watching the activities around the camp. We didn't know whether to approach the people and inform them of our plight. At some stage Mother said she was going to try to draw the attention of the villagers by hailing them. She changed her mind, however, fearing that her voice might echo and be heard by the enemy.

But unbeknown to us, the people's spies had long seen us and were waiting to see what our intentions were. As we stood thinking about what action to take, there was a stirring in the branches behind us. Fearing that we were being attacked by an animal, Mother took out her spear and readied herself to react. Before she could act on her fears, she was confronted by the appearance of a young man armed to the teeth.

I was so scared I was shaking like a leaf. He looked around as though checking the area and then greeted us in a kind voice, asking Mother: 'Who are you?'

'We are the Makhobas from the Shiyane mountain,' Mother answered. 'We are running away from the Redcoats.'

'Are you by yourselves or do you have other people with you?'

'It's only me and my children,' said Mother.

'Are you telling me the truth, woman?'

72

'Yes, I am. Look, these are my husband's weapons. He was killed at war. We haven't eaten in weeks and have been sleeping in trees, hiding from the animals and the invaders. We are destitute.'

'Come with me,' said the young man.

We followed him. He took us to the group of people we had spotted from where we had been hiding. They told us they, too, were survivors of the war and were led by a warrior called Ngebeza of the Hlabisa clan.

They were a vibrant community living in makeshift houses made out of grass and branches. They welcomed us and we told them our tale of sorrow and asked for food. They fed us. We had spent months living alone in the caves; now we were witnessing what seemed like a semblance of normal life. It was unbelievable. Being shown kindness and hospitality by complete strangers was humbling, particularly after what we had witnessed at the foot of the mountain where deserters had shown no compassion for their fellow men, the fallen warriors.

After we had eaten, an elderly woman, whom everybody addressed as Ndlunkulu (one of the leaders' wives) and who was clearly the matriarch, asked Mother to accompany her to meet the leader. She led us to a distinguished-looking elderly man to whom we were to introduce ourselves and by so doing pay the customary respect to him and his group.

With Mother holding our hands, we slowly approached the man who was seated away from the crowd. Not too far from him were a few young warriors who no doubt were his bodyguards. They stood at attention, holding their spears and shields. Their muscled arms were adorned with broad leafy white feathers. They were dressed in the traditional ibheshu, the cowhide apron worn by Zulu men.

The leader sat regally on a carved tree stump. He sat upright looking majestic, as though showing off his broad face with its large nose and broad lips. His cheeks were marked with the Usuthu traditional tribal lines and there were large button-like stoppers fixed to his dangling earlobes. His grey hair was enhanced by isicoco – the black rubber-like ring awarded by the king to outstanding warriors and worn with honour and pride. He sat with his head held high in a haughty sort of way, obviously conscious of his good looks and the power he wielded within the group. Like the young warriors guarding him, he too wore fine birds' feathers on his arms. His broad muscled chest displayed a necklace made out of animal teeth. To complete the regal look, a leopard skin was draped over one shoulder. There was no mistaking him for anything but a distinguished warrior.

We held tightly on to Mother's hands as she led us towards the man. When we were close to where he was seated, Mother motioned us to go down on our knees. The man had obviously been informed of our presence, and clearly had seen us approach him. We remained on our knees while he ignored us completely and carried on talking to the people next to him. We held our kneeling position with our eyes glued to the ground because custom dictated that we may not look a superior person in the eyes. My bones were hurting. I would gladly have paid any price to sit up but we had to maintain our position until the man acknowledged us.

This cold reception bothered me. I knew that it was customary for old people, particularly those in positions of importance, to take time to warm to strangers but this man was taking his importance to extremes. My father was an adviser to the king and a community leader and I had seen many people kneel before him. Those seeking counsel with my dad, particularly women, would accost my father by rattling off the family praise names while kneeling on the floor. My dad would immediately instruct Mother or whoever was nearby to bring the grass mat for the caller to sit on. If the caller was a man, then isigqiki, a stool, would be offered to him. Father never allowed anyone to be on their knees for longer than they had to. I was therefore taken aback by the behaviour of the leader who was ignoring our presence.

Later, when we had been accepted by the group, Mother confessed to me that there was a moment when she too had been worried about Ngebeza's reception of us. She told me that a thought had crossed her mind that we may have fallen among Zulus who had defected to the white people. If that was the case, with a name like Makhoba we could have been in trouble. My father was known near and far by both friends and foes of the king. He was a renowned warrior and had often been part of the delegation that met with Somtseu. Not too long ago he had been part of the group that had been sent by the king to broker a truce with Chelmsford. They were to deliver cattle and elephant tusks to Chelmsford who had accepted the gifts but declined the truce.

After what seemed like an eternity, Ngebeza's number one induna greeted us and then the leader began to pay attention to Mother. He wanted to know who we were and where we were from. Mother told him we were the Makhobas from the Shiyane mountains, across the uMzinyathi River.

'Do you know where you are?' he asked.

Mother shook her head.

'Do you know how far you are from your home? You have just

entered the Usuthu area. The river you have crossed is Vuna. You are not far from Nongoma.'

Suddenly, as if stung by some insect, the man raised his head and asked: 'Which Makhoba are you? Are you the wife of the adviser to the king? He comes from that part of the country, the great warrior of the iNgobamakhosi regiment? Hha! That is a fighter. The whole world knows of him.'

He uttered the words with pride and a smile, but when he looked at my mother, he noticed that she was crying. His happy countenance quickly disappeared. Seeing our mother crying, my sister and I joined her. Everyone was stunned and a pregnant silence descended on the group. As Mother cried, she kept pointing at the weapons that I was carrying. Nobody seemed to understand what she was saying. The elderly lady brought water and asked her to drink. Once she had calmed down, Mother spoke about our ordeal. How we had fled from our home and moved from mountain to mountain, from cave to cave, until we arrived here. She spoke of how we had found Father's weapons outside the entrance to the cave where we were hiding, and how we had fled from our hideout and come across a huge number of bodies covering the plain at the foot of the mountain.

'These are his weapons. He is no more.'

The man looked up and shook his head as if in denial.

'What are you telling me, woman? The king's adviser, the valiant Makhoba, is no more? The Zulu nation is finished. It's over with us. Our people are dead and their bodies scattered all over the mountains and the plains. It is over with uZulu.'

Once more an indescribable hush descended on the crowd. It was as though a calming breeze had breathed on to the group. The few elderly women in the group sniffed and suppressed their tears while the men shook their heads in anguish.

The man then asked Mother what her plans were. She told him we had nowhere to go, and asked if we could join his group.

'My children, all of us have nowhere to go. We have no homes, our villages have been burnt down and our fields pillaged. You are children of a great warrior. You are welcome to live with us. I, together with my brothers here, will look after you. We will give you food and water, and make you comfortable.'

★

We were embraced by the community and became part of them. The group was always on the move. We would camp at one place for a few days while the scouts travelled ahead of us to check the whereabouts of the enemy. Once the road was clear, we would pack up and leave. During the camping days, the men went hunting and the women and girls cooked the food. At night, the men watched over the group, taking turns to sleep. We travelled for months.

One afternoon we were joined by a group of warriors from Hlobane. They came with herds of cattle and foodstuffs. They told Ngebeza that they had been in a battle where they suffered defeat. Their general and the majority of the warriors were killed. They said the invaders had taken them as prisoners of war, leaving them under the guard of the African servants. In the middle of the night they had managed to overpower their guards, kill them all and take off with the cattle and alien foodstuffs such as flour, biscuits, tea, and a lot of tinned foodstuffs such as corned beef and fish.

Ngebeza welcomed them into the group. We kept the cattle but we destroyed and discarded the strange foodstuffs. A few cows were slaughtered and there were celebrations in our camp. It didn't matter that these men were strangers. What mattered was that they were Zulus and, like us, they needed a home and they had found us. They had brought cattle; they were a group of young men and brave fighters. They were very welcome.

Fearing that the white people would be on our trail, particularly as they had lost their cattle, Ngebeza decided that it was time we moved further into Zululand. He said we would have to cross the Mona River to an area where there was no white presence. The group had expanded, and this slowed our progress. The herds of cattle we had acquired slowed down our movements even more. There were also women with babies sired by the young warriors.

We travelled for nearly two weeks before we crossed the Mona River and settled down once more. We collected grass and began building huts. Ngebeza distributed the cattle equitably among the families and the memories of the war receded to the backs of our minds as we began to reconstruct our lives.

Mother, my sister and I realised how lucky we were to have come across the Ngebeza clan. They were kind people, full of hope and fun. We shared everything, food and chores alike. The community pooled their resources to build each family a hut. We shared the food and the milk that was available. The women with small children got the bulk of the milk. In the afternoons, while the women prepared dinner, the men went to the river and smoked dagga. They returned to the village intoxicated. They sang war songs and pranced about in merriment. But sometimes they came back from the river after smoking dagga in a melancholy mood and talked about nothing except the war. Their depressed mood affected all of us and then almost everyone began to reminisce about the war and what we had lost.

We had almost begun to accept the reasons for our hardships when one afternoon we were reminded of our fate by the arrival of a group of warriors. They said they had been at the battle of Khambula and that everyone else had perished. The worst piece of news was that they had been told that the king was dead.

They were taken to Ngebeza who questioned them at great length about the battle and the whereabouts of the king. They did not know much. They claimed to have managed to bypass Ulundi because of the presence of the invaders in the area. They said that as they went past Mahlabathini, they had seen smoke smouldering at the king's palace at Ondini.

They had been told by people they met on the road that the king was nowhere to be seen. We were later to learn that white people wearing red coats and white helmets had torched the king's palace. However, the ancestors were so incensed by that deed that the flames were unable to obliterate the buildings. Instead, the fire had smouldered for many days. Ngebeza opened his heart to the veterans and they, too, became part of our community.

With the new arrivals, the community was even bigger and dug its roots deeper into its new home. Couples got married and babies were born. Although we had not forgotten the members of our extended families from whom we had been separated, we gradually came to terms with the fact we might never see them again. By now I had accepted that my father was dead. He was, however, an ever-present memory in my mind.

One afternoon Ngebeza summoned Mother to his kraal. She was told to bring us along. Our knees shaking with apprehension, we set off for the induna's kraal. On the way to the meeting, Mother told us that she was worried because she did not know why we had been summoned. In Zululand it was a common practice for people who were suspected of felonies, such as practising witchcraft or being unruly and making life difficult for others, to be summoned to the kraal where they would be tried and sentenced. The messenger from the induna had said nothing to her beyond the fact that Ngebeza wanted to see her and her children.

We arrived at the kraal where we found the entire male population of the village congregated. A few elderly women were also present together with uNdlunkulu, the first lady. Ngebeza smiled when he saw us. We knelt next to uNdlunkulu, and waited for Ngebeza to address us.

'I see you, my children,' he said. 'Please sit down and make yourselves comfortable.'

Those were not the words of an angry person and I was convinced that we were not in trouble. We sat down and stretched out our legs, assuming a comfortable sitting position and waiting to be told why we had been called to appear before the induna. In Zulu culture, as a sign of respect, women and children do not look elderly people, or those in positions of authority, in the eyes. They keep their eyes glued to the ground. As we sat there I began to speculate about the reason we had been called to the kraal and surreptitiously I looked at the people gathered there. As I did so, I thought my eyes were playing tricks on me because seated next to Ngebeza was my uncle, Makhoba Omkhulu. I had not realised how much my uncle looked like my father. The similarity was uncanny. I could almost have sworn that the man seated next to Ngebeza was my dad. My father always grew a beard and so did my uncle.

Just then Mother clapped her hands and exclaimed, 'Am I dreaming? Am I sleeping? Are you Makhoba Omkhulu? Brother, is it really you?' She could not contain her excitement. Folding her arms and hands over her head, tears of joy cascaded down her cheeks.

Makhoba Omkhulu smiled and said, 'Yes, it's me.'

I jumped up and went over to him. I kissed him, hugged him and cried. He held me tight against his chest and stroked my head. I told him how happy I was he had found us. The induna motioned me to sit down. I sat on my uncle's knee and was quiet. Then Ngebeza addressed the assembly.

'People of the king, I have called you to this meeting because of this man before you. He has travelled all the way from the Great uMzinyathi looking for his children. To those who are wondering who he is, he is Makhoba from the Shiyane mountain. I am sure you are familiar with that area for it is next to Isandlwana, the little hill that looks like a hut where the brave Zulu warriors taught the invaders a lesson. His brother Umgqokotshwa was one of the brave fighters who killed many of the invaders at the battle of Isandlwana.'

Ngebeza lifted his right hand, gathering his thumb and first three fingers together into a fist, except for the pinky finger, and gesticulating as though he was stabbing the air, said: 'Buka, umlungu.' Look, this is what he did to the white man. Each time he stabbed the air with his small finger he would say, 'Buka, umlungu.'

Ngebeza was pleased with himself as he narrated the incident using his pinky finger, a symbol of the spear which the Zulus used to stab and kill with.

'Umgqokotshwa died in battle. His brother has been looking for his children. I am glad that he has found them. You are free to take your family and go.'

It was my uncle's turn to speak.

'Where do I begin to thank you for looking after my children? I've searched all over for them. There was a time when I thought maybe they had been killed by the marauding invaders or by the wild animals who have since acquired the taste for human flesh. Somehow something told me not to give up looking for them. I am so grateful to you, Nduna. I am sure that even my brother, wherever his spirit is, is happy. I am going to take them home.'

I watched my uncle speak. At that moment, it was as if my father was living within Makhoba Omkhulu. He had transformed into my father and it made me both happy and sad.

Ngebeza answered my uncle's speech of gratitude with an invitation. He said: 'It would give me great pleasure if you could spend the day with us and take the children tomorrow.'

He ordered the slaughter of a number of cattle, beer flowed and the festivities began. Our farewell party went on until the early hours of the morning. Although the Ngebeza community was sad that we were leaving, they were happy to celebrate our reunion with our uncle. With tears rolling down our cheeks, my mother, Ndumbutshu and I departed for home the next day, leaving behind families and friends who had taken us in and accepted us as their own.

*

When Sis Ahh had finished telling the story, there was not a single dry eye in the room and the time was long past midnight.

PART THREE

Adrift

Habisa has a peculiar climate. The villages are surrounded by little hills and mountains and the area experiences frequent rainfall and gale-force winds. However, the trees and buildings in Sis Ahh's yard go a long way in protecting the homestead against the harsh climate. Sis Ahh and I enjoyed working outside behind the main house, not far from the graveyard where members of her family, including her husband, fondly known as Mshibe, lie. I sat on the bench holding the tape recorder and my notebook and she sat on the grass mat with her feet stretched out before her. Often we would be served lunch outside.

That afternoon was not a good day for us. Sis Ahh, who suffers from diabetes, was experiencing pain emanating from a lesion between her toes. She was gently rubbing medicine onto her wound. I became curious about the jar containing the solution or ointment and I asked her: 'What ointment is that? Let me have a look.'

She grabbed the little tin and as she was extending it to me she said: 'It's python fat. It is good for healing wounds.' I was about to take the tin but her answer stopped me in my tracks.

'Where do you get the fat of a python?' I asked her in wonderment.

'Oh, that! There are many snakes around here,' she said. You just have to tell the boys herding the cattle to get you the fat. Here you are, smell it. It has no smell and it is rich in nutrients.'

This was creepy. I began looking around where I was sitting. I didn't want to

87

touch the tin. I had an uneasy feeling, as though pythons were slithering towards me in large numbers. I became angry with my sister. She knew how scared I was of snakes and yet she blithely let me know that she was applying snake fat to her feet. Not just an ordinary snake, a python. Maybe she was joking?

In an effort to elicit the truth from her I asked her: 'And you expect me to sleep in your house tonight where there is snake fat?'

'Are you scared that the snake will come to get its fat? Don't be silly, township girl. Nothing will happen to you. We will sleep well like we always do.'

'Tell me, how do you, as a nurse who has been practising modern medicine, turn around and use this mumbo-jumbo witchcraft stuff?'

'What?' she laughed, rolling her big eyes and displaying her near-toothless smile. 'You call this witchcraft. You know nothing about witchcraft, and even less about your so-called Western medicine. What do you think some of the Western medicine is made of? Do you know what constitutes penicillin? Do you know that it is made out of a mould? Nothing fancy, my dear girl, and resourced from the natural environment. Do you know the medicinal value of dagga? And have you ever heard of leech treatment, how the tiny ugly water worms are unleashed on a wound to suck the blood to cure the disease? Snake fat is used in a number cures. Cosmetic products that you town people love to apply to your skin, some of their ingredients are from parts of snakes.'

Her reply not only confused me, it shut me up. Later in the day, her house-keeper brought us lunch. She had prepared roast pork, spinach and boiled sweet potatoes. There is no sweet potato like the one grown in Zululand. The ones we get from the supermarkets in Johannesburg are stringy and wet and lack sweet-ness. Zululand sweet potato is dry and very sweet. My plate of food looked mouth-watering. I was about to start eating when I suddenly remembered that we had not been to the shops lately so we should not be having meat. In fact, I had been thinking of going to the shops later that day to replenish some of the items we had run short of, and meat was on top of my shopping list.

'When did you get this meat?' I asked her.

'My gosh, don't you ever get tired of inquisitions? One of my neighbours slaughtered a pig and he gave me some meat,' she answered.

'Are you sure this meat has no tapeworm?' I asked, thinking back to the 1950s when there was a tapeworm plague in black areas. I recalled watching semi-clad piccaninnies from the township squatting in the open veld relieving themselves and seeing live white worms that looked like small buttons crawling out of the little mounds left by the township toddlers. The thought made my skin crawl.

'Sorry, Sis, I'll pass on the meat. I'll have the spinach and the sweet potato.'

'You are incredible, you know! First it was the snake, now it's the tapeworm. What will it be next?' she said, laughing at me while she dug into her food. I joined her in eating but I did not touch the meat.

The day turned out to be depressing because we were dealing with a difficult chapter. Sis Ahh explained that Gogo told her that although the war between the English and Zulus was over, another battle had begun – the battle for human survival.

'At that stage, Gogo's father was dead,' said Sis Ahh. 'And so was his mother, our great-grandmother. There were many people they knew who had died. Some had fallen in battle, others had been too old and frail to survive the war and its ramifications, and they had perished.'

We lapsed into silence as Gogo's story took centre stage once more ...

★

The sight of young widows carrying babies and struggling to make ends meet was a common one. The babies had big skeletal heads and distended stomachs, symptoms of kwashiorkor, a disease afflicting malnourished young children. Also common was the sight of starving elderly men and women. These skin-and-bone figures were seen wandering along the paths, trying to eke out a living in the wilderness.

The effects of starvation were more visible on the men. The ibheshu, the leather apron worn by men that covered the front and back, did little to hide the scrawny legs. It was difficult to reconcile this sight with the memory of the once-proud warriors whose muscular legs had carried them up and down the cliffs and the valleys of Zululand, singing war songs and stomping their way into battle. These were the men who had pranced and exclaimed 'ngadla mina', a war cry which denotes victory, as they plunged their spears into the bodies of their foes. Those were the days when they thought and felt they were invincible. They were now reduced to beggars; homeless and landless, roaming the plains and mountains of Zululand looking for food and somewhere to lay their heads.

The lack of proper nutrition was also apparent on the young maidens, scantily clad in pieces of hide that looked like skirts but only hid their private parts, together with the strings of beads that covered their breasts. Much as they tried to present an intrepid exterior in the face of hunger and deprivation, their once shining and healthy-looking ebony skin was now taut and looked set to crack at any moment. Their cheeks, sunburnt and peeling, covered by skin whose veneer sprouted tiny strands of hair, a sure sign of malnutrition.

Nor had the elderly women escaped the hardships brought about by the war. They shuffled around the plateaus and the valleys in their tattered leather skirts and ibhayi that covered their shrivelled breasts and stomachs. These women searched everywhere for something to feed their dependants on. They dug the barren soil in vain. These were the same women who in the olden days would accompany their men to battle, prance, dance and ululate while the men fought it out. With the current war, they were not in a position to witness the battles because the enemy their men were fighting used weapons that could kill from miles away.

Many wounded warriors who had survived the battles died of starvation. Also gone were the hardy Nguni cattle that could withstand bad weather; cows that delivered milk even in the drought season. With the arable land along the rivers now occupied by the foreigners, the Zulu people were banished to the barren parts of the region.

Some men and women of the older generation were convinced that the cause of the tragedy was a curse laid on the whole nation by the ancestors as a punishment for the assassination of King Shaka. They were convinced that the ancestors had turned their backs on the Zulu nation and they believed the answer to the problem lay in the nation's atoning for the evil deed committed by King Shaka's brothers Dingane and Mhlangana. There was a need for a cleansing ceremony in order to appease the ancestors. But without cattle to slaughter for such a ritual, and no king to give orders and direct the performance of this ceremony, nothing could be done. The nation was desperate.

For those who had not surrendered to the foreigners, not knowing the whereabouts of King Cetshwayo was a great source of pain. They knew that their existence was doomed without the knowledge of what had happened to their king.

The entire nation, including the people who had deserted to the white folk, were worried about the disappearance of the king which led to the many stories being told about the king's whereabouts. Some of them said their masters swore they had seen a thin-looking king, with a sagging belly, captured and taken to the country where the foreigners came from. Others, also living on white farms, said their masters had told them that King Cetshwayo had been captured and killed and his remains were fed to the wild animals.

The ravages of war were visible everywhere. The landscape had not been spared: the once-green fields of Zululand lay bare. Where nutritional vegetation once grew wild, nothing but useless brown bushes remained. The rivers had run dry. The few streams with flowing water were contaminated with all kinds of toxic waste making it unsafe for human consumption. People survived on fountains that occasionally spouted water. The land, once dotted with cattle and goats, showed no signs of life. Thousands of cattle had died of some unknown disease.

And yet across the escarpment where the white people had settled, life was a hive of activity and increasing prosperity. The Zulu people watched with anger and pain beating in their hearts as farm after farm sprang up along the uMzinyathi area and in the verdant valleys around Dundee, Utrecht and Eshowe. White people had settled in the best parts of Zululand and the Zulu people were relegated to the outskirts of the country, the Mahlabathini, Nongoma and Mkhuze areas around the Black and White uMfolozi Rivers. Daily, wagons traversed the land carrying foodstuffs and appliances. The white people were constructing houses and installing irrigation systems that brought water to their farms. Increasing numbers of white people were arriving and settling on the land where they were assisted by those who had already made their homes there. AmaZulu watched helplessly as the land of Mthaniya was transformed into a foreign settlement where they were only welcome as labourers.

The Zulu people who had deserted during the war were now white people's servants. They worked alongside the white man carrying the heavy stuff needed for the creation and the establishment of the new settlements. Strong Zulu men and women worked in the fields and the younger women and girls worked in the houses, cooking and cleaning. The same happened to the people who had been abducted by the invaders during the war. They too had been turned into farm workers, earning a pittance if, indeed, they earned anything at all. Some of the white people were benevolent enough to allow their servants to keep cattle on the farms and even offered them some land for their own use. This was done on the clear understanding that the land belonged to the white master. Other farmers allowed their workers to come and go, particularly during winter season when there was no farming.

Of the many problems we faced, the capitulation of some of the Zulus to the white people was the biggest and the most distressing to deal with.

Those of us who had remained true to the king, even in his absence, we who had stuck to the nation and its values were concerned about the future of uZulu. There was no gainsaying that the Zulu nation was now divided; there was nothing to prevent its demise. Those of us who still owed allegiance to the king were concerned about how and who was going to reconstruct the nation when we were so divided. We were in desperate need of some glue to keep us together. For a young nation founded by King Shaka in the 1820s, barely fifty years old, the disappearance of the king and the division did not augur well for us. It was hurtful to see the efforts of our forefathers, who built the nation with sweat and blood, go to waste. It was sad to see a nation that was respected all over Africa disintegrate and go up in smoke, all because of greed. Why did the invaders want everything? Surely there was enough for all of us.

We were also concerned about the transformation the deserters had undergone. They had not only turned their backs on the Zulu nation, they had become complete aliens. Their lifestyle and mannerisms had turned them into strange creatures. To start with, they no longer dressed like us. The men did not wear ibheshu any more. They now walked about in long baggy trousers and overcoats that were too big for them. Most of this apparel was handed down to them either from dead soldiers or from their masters. They looked comical as they trudged around or worked in the fields in their unwieldy outfits. If their trousers were not over-long then they were too short, reaching just below the knee. As if that was not enough, the men were made to shave off the isicoco, the coveted black head ring bestowed by the king on warriors who had displayed extraordinary fighting prowess.

The women were not exempted. Our traditional clothing consisted of a leather skirt and ibhayi, a large cloth which was draped over the shoulders and knotted across the chest. This cloth covered the entire body from the shoulders, reaching to just below the knee, back and front. The women who worked in the white people's homes were made to wear long, cumbersome skirts which covered them from head to toe, and they had to perform arduous tasks such as cleaning floors, preparing meals and even working in the fields in these heavy flowing skirts. They were at the beck and call of their master and mistress at any given moment. Their husbands had no say in what they did; they were now the invaders' property. They worked long hours compared to us who only had to work in our fields, cook dinner and busy ourselves with handwork such as making grass mats or plaiting each other's hair. Like the men, the women were told to shave off their hair and remove the inhloko, the broad headgear worn by married women. Occasionally we would come across some of the women at the river washing their clothes. We sympathised with them because those of us who had not defected to the white people didn't have clothing to wash. Our traditional skirts were made out of animal skin which required no washing.

One of the questions that puzzled us was why the foreigners were obsessed with ensuring that our people covered their bodies. Why did they want to impose their clothing on us? Why couldn't they let us be? We were quite comfortable in our animal-hide apparel and we went about the daily business of staying alive semi-naked. Some of the deserters told us that the problem with our lack of clothing lay with the white women who couldn't bear to witness the sculpted sinewy naked bodies and well-tanned skins of their workers. The sight of healthy-looking black bodies disturbed their sensibilities. This was baffling to us because we didn't attach much importance to our physical appearance. Of course we adorned our bodies with all types of paraphernalia such as beads and feathers but beyond that our bodies were just meant to perform certain duties. For instance, young maidens walked about semi-naked, with their breasts in full view. This was not to evoke sexual or amorous emotions. Breasts were for feeding babies and there was no need to hide them, nor was there any need to hide the muscular thighs of young men wearing ibheshu. A friend who had lost her family during the war and was now living with white people on the neighbouring farm came to visit me. I noticed she was wearing a strange string of beads around her neck. I asked her what it was and where her African beads were. She told me she had stopped wearing the 'heathen' beads because they were demonic. What she had on were church beads called a 'rosary'. It had been given to her by the church people when she converted to Christianity.

She started to tell me about the virtues of the church and how fulfilled her life had been since she became a Christian. She had abandoned the devil worship of dead people and was now worshipping a living God. I wanted to know who these Christian people were and where they came from. Were they not the same foreigners who had killed many of our people? She told me that the ones who had converted her to Christianity were not the Redcoats. They were church people who had come to our land to save us from the devil, so that we could go to heaven when we died. I could not believe my ears. There was now another set of white people who had come to save us. A few months back they were killing us, now they were saving us. I was livid. I had flashbacks of the numerous incidents that had happened to me and to many people I knew. Now this girl who was living with the people who had taken and destroyed our lives expected me to embrace them. I was convinced the white people had bewitched her.

I asked her to tell me more about heaven and hell because I believed that when I died I would join my ancestors and all the people who had died before me. I knew that they would welcome me and rejoice at my arrival. I couldn't understand that there was another place called hell which was worse than what we were experiencing in our daily lives. What could be more hell than to be stripped of your worth, your king, your nationhood and your land? How much more hell was there than being a slave?

The deserters' new dress code which clearly separated us from them was not the only problem. There was an even more serious issue between us. The deserters had an attitude towards us. They carried themselves in such a haughty fashion that they had even developed a new terminology. They called themselves Amakholwa, the believers, and they referred to us as Amabhinca, those who wore ibhayi and animal hides. Even the manner in which they said the word Amabhinca was full of contempt and they talked about us in terms that made us seem inferior to them.

Their strange behaviour was worse at funerals. When attending a funeral of one of us who had not capitulated to white ways, the Amakholwa would take over the proceedings and impose their Christian practices on us. We watched and listened to them sing songs we did not know about a world hereafter, a world we had never heard of.

The ritual was worse when one of them, a believer, was buried. They went overboard with this worship stuff and spoke ad infinitum about the person who had died, extolling his or her virtues and condemning those who had not converted to Christianity. They would go on and tell those of us who were clinging to our Zulu beliefs how we were going to be condemned to burn in hell. Oh, how sanctimonious they were as they sang the strange songs eulogising some unseen person! They would go on for hours, much to our disbelief and annoyance.

The Amakholwa made death a fearful event, where the departed spirit would wander about restlessly for years. At worst, the dead would descend into hell where there was gnashing of teeth and the burning of flesh. For us non-Christians, death was a journey towards being reunited with those who had died before us. We would bid the deceased farewell, through him send greetings to our ancestors, asking them to protect us. We saluted our forefathers, calling them by name, one by one, to receive whoever was being buried. To us, death was not the end of a journey but a continuation of life where one would join kinsfolk who had gone before us.

There was nothing to fear about dying. For instance, I saw dying as a time when I would be united with my father and my grandmother. I visualised arriving at a particular place where departed people were reposing, the men on one side and the women on the other. When I reached this holy ground someone would say: 'Oh! Nombhosho, daughter of Makhoba, you have come at last. Give her some beer to drink before she meets her grandparents.' After taking a big gulp of beer, I would be ushered to my grandmother who would be in the company of other old women. Later I would be escorted to where my father and the rest of the men were. I would be welcomed with dance and song. I always envisaged death as a happy reunion. I could not imagine going to a place where I would be accosted by guards and someone reading a long list of the wrongs I had committed while I was alive.

Attending a wedding of the Amakholwa was another such debilitating experience. Their weddings did away with most of the traditional activities associated with Zulu weddings. We were used to festivities and merriment that went on for days, where cows and goats would be slaughtered and beer would flow. Our traditional Zulu wedding 'umgcagco' was a celebration of life, where people were entertained in accordance with their rank. The local maidens would converge on the bride's parental home where they would be treated to sumptuous meals before eventually accompanying the bride to her new home. The people attending the wedding would be fed according to hierarchy. The elderly women dined separately from the younger ones, and were served specially selected cuts of meat deserving of venerable members of the community.

The older men of the village had a special place set aside for them. Like the elderly women, they too were served with selected pieces of meat and with large calabashes of beer. The young men, the groom's peers, were attended to separately and the herdboys were also given special attention. The festivities lasted for days until all the traditional rituals that had to be conducted were concluded and it was time for the delegation to accompany the bride to her new home. But not before the family elders had talked to her, outlining to her the rules and regulations of marriage; what she should do and not do. Top of the list was to inform her that leaving her father's homestead was the detachment of the umbilical cord, the final goodbye. Under no circumstances was she to return home. Other rules concerned behaving with respect towards everything at her new home and showing subservience to her in-laws. The most popular advice was often phrased in this manner: 'If you find that your in-laws are witches, then you must join them and be the best witch.'

On arrival at the groom's homestead, the people accompanying the bride were treated to good food and beer. Here as well the wedding festivities continued for days marked by song and dance competitions between the groom's and the bride's entourages. The bride handed out gifts to members of the groom's family and she was inducted into the ways of her new home. In the meantime, outside in the open veld, young men engaged in stick fights. It was a common sight to see young men bleeding from wounds sustained during the fighting as grudges and scores were often settled during the wedding celebrations. Young maidens and young men were offered the time of their lives, as there was ample opportunity to mingle during the singing and dancing and the eating and drinking. Liaisons between young people were often initiated during this time, and just as many hearts were broken.

By contrast, Christian weddings were dull and brief. The couple met in church where a priest or church elder – someone wearing a serious look, as if officiating at a funeral – would conduct the ceremony. He would address the couple and tell them how to behave themselves in marriage. We found this insulting because we had structures that prepared both girls and boys for the various stations in life. The izinkehli and amaqhikiza – the older and unmarried girls – were the custodians of good behaviour and morality among the girls as they grew up. They were also responsible for teaching the girls about their bodies. Matters such as what to do when with a lover were handled by these women. They taught the girls how to avoid falling pregnant by practising ukusoma, that is, not to let the boy penetrate the girl but instead to play around the thighs. Our aunts and mothers dealt with matters such as how to run a household, stressing particularly the respect that should be shown towards the husband and all members of his family, including showing love and respect for the babies born to the sisters of the husband. Our fathers and uncles were responsible for imparting values to the groom. With Christian weddings, after the priest had given instructions of what had to be done in a marriage, the bride was whisked away to her new home where celebrations lasted for that day only.

★

In the absence of the king, the white people were in total authority. To rub salt in our wounds, they introduced onongqayi, policemen. The concept of policing a community was alien to us. Communities knew the dos and don'ts. We did not have prisons in which to keep wrong-doers. The king and his councillors were the judge and jury. Members of the village did participate in the trial, adding a voice of caution and suggestions; otherwise the entire trial was in the hands of the king. If the offender was found guilty of a felony such as stock theft, he was punished, usually with a slap on the wrist in the form of a fine. If the crime was of a serious nature such as murder, the miscreant was killed on the spot and that was the end of the matter.

We had never heard of people called onongqayi; they were a creation of the invaders. They went about arresting local people for misdemeanours such as injuring a neighbour during a stick fight, or sniffing out witches. The concept of policing the community was not only foreign, it was anathema. We did not even have a name for it; nongqayi was part of the new terminology that the Amakholwa had developed.

So many things had gone wrong and yet there were people, like my friend with her stupid-looking string of beads, who extolled the virtues of the church people and their strange behaviour. My friend was one of the many who had been displaced from her community and was living in a white home and working for them and being paid with a string of beads that were not even as colourful as ours. The sad part was that she was not the only one who believed in this mumbo-jumbo. There were many like her. Some of them were grey-haired men and women who should have known better.

There were many Zulus who thought and behaved like my friend. These people had turned their backs on the king and all he stood for and they now looked up to their masters as their leaders. They had abandoned ancestral worship and embraced white traditions and looked down on African customs. They informed us that they had been converted to a new kind of worship and were attending church services. When we enquired what happened at this thing they called 'church', they told us they sang songs and prayed to the strangers' deities which they now believed in. What had happened to uMvelinqangi, our god? The white people had eclipsed uMvelinqangi and replaced him with uNkulunkulu in the same way they had nudged us out of our abodes.

Very little of this made sense to me. What was worse was the manner in which the deserters conducted themselves, particularly towards us. They were arrogant and carried themselves as if they still owned the land they walked on whereas, like us, they had lost everything. Even their souls were owned by the whites they worked for. I often wondered how different their worship was from ours. Our sangomas and divine healers also held sacred meetings where they conferred with the departed and asked for guidance. They often came together to exchange ideas about how to practise their calling to get rid of evil spirits that might harm members of the community. Now these Christian converts had the nerve to look down on us as if what the invaders had introduced them to was of a higher standing.

I could not understand how these people who had defected could trust the strangers to the extent of undergoing such a change themselves. It was not as if they did not know what these people were capable of. Like us, they had lived through the war and had witnessed the assault on the entire nation. Yet they had undergone a complete about-turn. They were no longer a part of us. Had they really forgotten what we went through at the hands of the invaders?

★

The war ended while we were in hiding. We were separated from our relatives and everyone we knew. We were clueless about the activities of the war and knew even less about the whereabouts of our family, until the morning Makhoba Omkhulu came looking for us and took us back home. This time home was not the foothills of the Shiyane mountains. My uncle told us that Zulu people no longer lived in that part of the country; that land now belonged to the foreigners. Our home was in a small community at Nquthu, an arid uncultivatable place with lots of stones. In our wanderings around Zululand, I had never come across such a stony landscape. It was as though the entire area was a stone plantation. There were big boulder-like stones and small smooth-surfaced ones, and they were everywhere.

The reunion with members of our family was a joyful event. Everybody was happy to see us and commented on how much we had grown up. My cousins had grown to be beautiful teenagers; they were now fully developed and entering adulthood. A big feast was held, beer was brewed and a goat was slaughtered to give thanks to the ancestors for protecting and preserving us during the war. It was a wonderful day for all of us. Some of the neighbours joined in the celebration and as the beer flowed stories about the war were shared. People spoke of the difficulties they had experienced having to survive, as we had to, on roots and rats.

'There were times when we lived in places that were so dry that nothing came out of the ground, there were no roots to unearth,' said one of my aunts. 'At those times we would eat mud.'

'And what about the diarrhoea after that?' remarked another aunt.

Makhoba Omkhulu added his voice to the narrative, speaking of how he had walked for days looking for us.

'I went from village to village, asking people if they had come across a woman with two small children. Sometimes people took pity on me, fed me and gave me a place to sleep. I would be up first thing in the morning to continue my search. Others told me of their own problems. At times I felt I was being a nuisance, that I was burdening people with my problems when they had their own to deal with. One could see the pain of loss in the eyes of some of the people I spoke to. Wherever I went, people talked of their ordeal, of what they had lost.

'Then one day I came across a man who was a nongqayi. At first I didn't want to talk to him but for some strange reason I found myself pouring out my problems to him. He was very sympathetic and told me to go across the Vuna and the Mona Rivers and search around there. He said there was a new settlement of people who had survived the war. I took his advice and walked towards the north of Zululand. I felt lucky I had met this fellow because obviously I had all along been looking for my children in the wrong places. It took me another two days and nights to find you.'

MaNgubane, the senior aunt and wife to Makhoba Omkhulu related, in great detail, how Grandmother had fallen ill and died and how they had buried her somewhere in the mountains. It was a consolation to me to hear that they were at least able to bury her, unlike Father whose grave was unknown to us. We didn't even know if he had been buried at all. Maybe his end was similar to that of the many warriors whose corpses lay strewn over the plains of Zululand; bodies that invariably ended up in the stomachs of the vultures. I often wondered how and where he had died. In the silent conversations I often held with myself, I would talk to him and ask him questions such as 'Do you miss us?' or 'Are you really dead?'

When our turn came to speak, mother shared with them accounts of our sojourns in the various caves and how we spent every minute thinking about them and wondering if they were dead or alive. She ended her sad recital with the discovery of Father's weapons at the entrance of the cave where we were living.

'At first I didn't believe they were his arms,' she told them. 'I silently hoped there was a mistake, that one day he would return. As you all know, he never did. Someone told us that he took over Mbilini's regiments and was killed at the battle of Hlobane. I guess we will never know the truth of what happened to my husband.'

After the festivities, when everybody had gone back to their homes, I joined Mother on the grass mat where she was sleeping. What a day it had been. It felt so good to be back home with my family and it was wonderful to be welcomed by my cousins and aunts. It didn't matter to me that the new home was a far cry from our original home below the Shiyane mountains, next to the river whose banks were replete with all kinds of wild fruit and wild vegetables like imbuya – the wild green vegetable that looks like miniature spinach. I was so happy to be among my relatives and was looking forward to starting a new life.

In retrospect, however, I know that I suspected that there was someone who was not happy to see us return to the fold.

It didn't take me long to realise that life at our new homestead was not going to be easy. It was so different from our former home. Before the war we lived in a fertile region, not far from the uMzinyathi River, a place where everyone in the village had cattle and plenty to eat. The area was fertile enough for us to plant anything and to feed the cows and goats. Between my father and his two brothers, the Makhoba family had over sixty head of cattle. My father owned twenty-two cattle and fifteen goats. My job was to look after the goats. As their goatherd, I knew each and every one of them. There was always both fresh and sour milk. We had hectares and hectares of land on which we toiled to produce food. Our barns were bursting with stored maize and sorghum.

Then the war came and we lost everything: our loved ones, our king, our livestock, our land and our dignity. Now, as vanquished people, we had become the laughing stock of the invaders. They reminded us at every opportunity how they had beaten us in battle, and how Zululand now belonged to the Queen of England. What we couldn't understand was how these strange-looking men, people who could shoot and kill a human being from a long distance away, could be ruled by a woman. We found it bizarre that a woman could be responsible for sending able-bodied men from her country to Zululand to kill for her. What powers did this woman, whom the men called Queen, possess? And why was she so bloodthirsty that so many people had to die in her honour? In my country it would have been impossible for a woman to make men perform the deeds that these invaders had committed, unless she was a witch. Even Princess Mkabayi, King Shaka's aunt, who was the most powerful female member of the royal house, had not commanded the powers that the English queen seemed to have.

Our people had nothing. Many, particularly the old and infirm, were dying from hunger. There were no cattle, as most had been seized by the white people. The cattle we had tried to hide in the mountains had disappeared. The few that had survived were attacked by a disease and died. Without cows to milk and fields to grow food, there was famine in the land. The terrain was unsafe with wild animals roaming about in search of food. They had now acquired a taste for human flesh and people were attacked and killed. Many warriors had come back from the war maimed or crippled. The inyangas and muthi people were doing a roaring business dishing out potions of medicine to heal the injured. The ones with superficial wounds survived but many, particularly the ones with broken limbs or with bullets lodged in their bodies, died.

With Father dead, there was no news about the enemy. When he was alive we were privy to all kinds of information, even top state secrets because he was one of the king's advisers and spent most of his time at Ondini. With him gone, we were dependent on rumours, or on bits and pieces of information from the people who worked for the whites.

Those of us who lived in the reserves, the name given to native areas, were occasionally visited by the deserters. They came even though they knew how much we despised them. They also knew how impoverished we were. Needing to salvage their consciences, the farm workers brought us food. Living in the white homes enabled them to be better informed than us about current affairs. They told us that the king had been kidnapped by the white people, but they did not know where he had been taken to. There was much speculation about the whereabouts of the king. Some said the whites had abducted and killed him and fed his remains to the vultures. There were others who swore that they had seen the king and his wives fleeing to Swaziland.

We wanted to know what had happened to the king. He was the nation's treasure and his disappearance impacted catastrophically on the people. If the invaders had killed the king and used his remains as a potion to strengthen their dominion over us, it could have unspeakable consequences for the Zulu nation. The invaders did not believe in our ways, yet there was nothing to stop them from experimenting by forcing a sangoma to use the king's remains on the white people to reinforce their hold on us. The king had to be found, dead or alive.

The king's disappearance caused great consternation throughout the land. That, coupled with the settlers' takeover was worse than dying. It struck at the core of our existence. We had no king and there were no regiments. There were too many questions we needed answers for. Top of the list was the question of what was to happen to our traditions and practices since our ways clashed with those of the foreigners. We wanted to know what would happen to the annual festival of the yielding of the first fruits. How were we to thank uMvelinqangi for delivering food to us? Who would summon the nation to travel to the sacred mountain to give thanks to the Creator for the first crops of the season? What was to happen to the boys once they reached manhood since there was no regiment they could join? How would we honour the girls when they came of age? We feared that the celebration of our traditions and the practices of our culture would incur Somtseu's wrath, yet we couldn't imagine how we would survive without them. Without the king in charge to give us direction, what would happen to uZulu?

There was no joy in the land. People walked about with heavy hearts. We learned that Somtseu had retired and that his son had taken over. He was known as Misjan. Like his father, the young Misjan had announced at the end of the war that all the regiments were to be disbanded. In place of the king, thirteen chiefs were installed. These chiefs were not to govern the Zulu nation but to police the people on behalf of the Queen of England. Our nation was lost and divided, angry and helpless. There were those who swore they would never accede to a foreign leader or to the chiefs. They would rather be shot and killed before they bowed to Misjan's lackeys, while others resigned themselves to being ruled by Misjan and his puppets.

*

I had frequent nightmares. In the worst of them I was walking amidst dead bodies strewn all over the plains. Sometimes I had pleasant dreams during which my father visited me. We would go hunting and he would tell me that he would be coming home as soon as the war was over. I would wake up in high spirits and tell Mother my dream.

Once we were through with the pleasantries of being reunited with the family, we began reconstructing our lives. There was a lot to be done, starting with the building of a hut and barns. Even though we did not have cows, we put together logs to build a kraal in the hope that one day we might have cattle again for, as they say, hope springs eternal in the human breast.

Makhoba Omkhulu was most supportive of us. He organised an ilima, which is an African tradition whereby the community pools its resources to assist a family perform a much-needed task such as building a hut or a kraal or hoeing a field. On completion of the work for which they had congregated, the group spends the rest of the day drinking beer together.

Mother went calmly about her business of rebuilding our lives. Not once did she speak about our father. Sometimes at night I would see her fiddling with his weapons as though inspecting them. She kept them neat, safely tucked away. Makhoba Omkhulu spent a great deal of time in our hut. Sometimes he visited after he had been drinking with his friends and then he was usually in a jovial mood and entertained us with his storytelling.

Sometimes Mother brewed beer and Makhoba Omkhulu invited some of the neighbours to come and drink beer at our hut. Every time he slaughtered an animal, he personally brought meat to our hut and every morning he sent a boy to our hut with a can full of milk. He was one of the few in the village, apart from those who had relatives in white homes, who had a cow. He had somehow managed to secure a cow from the Africans working on the farms. He did everything in his power to help us settle. Of course I missed my father, but Makhoba Omkhulu tried to fill his place in looking after us and I was grateful.

The one thing that marred the happy picture was the peculiar behaviour of his wife, MaNgubane. From the outset she made it clear to everyone that she was not happy to have us back. She was not rude or discourteous towards us but she kept a noticeable distance and she hardly ever came to visit us. At some stage I wanted to ask my mother if she knew why Mamkhulu MaNgubane seldom came to our hut but decided against it because I knew she would not be pleased with me dabbling in adult matters. I was almost certain that if I had asked her, her answer, if any at all, would be 'that porridge is not meant for you'; in English it means 'that is none of your business'.

Strangely, Mother was not unlike MaNgubane in that she hardly visited anyone either. It had been different when my grandmother, her mother-in-law, was alive. Mother had always treated her as a friend. With Father away a lot of the time, Mother, who was the youngest of the wives, spent a great deal of time with the old lady, much to the envy and sometimes annoyance of the other women in the homestead. Mother would cook and take food to her. Most of what she knew about domestic management she had learned from her mother-in-law. She had been shown how to look after the home, how to brew beer, as well as how to raise children. She had been taught all that and more by the old lady. I was told that Mother was still very young when she got married and her mom had pleaded with Father's mother to take care of her baby 'because she is still so small'. Now, with Grandmother gone, Mother had no friends and therefore kept to herself.

Soon a rumour began circulating through the family that Makhoba Omkhulu was going to be our father. I did not understand what that meant because he had always been our father. Even when Father was alive Makhoba Omkhulu had treated us as his children and so had my father behaved towards Makhoba Omkhulu's children. We had always been a big happy family. In retrospect, I realised that I was too young to notice if Omkhulu had amorous feelings for Mother. Even if he hadn't, marrying Mother would not have raised any eyebrows for it was an accepted custom in the Zulu culture for a brother to ngena, which means to marry his brother's widow.

I spent a great deal of time with my cousins. We did almost everything together, from gathering wood in the forest to drawing water from the river. Yet lately I had noticed a change, particularly with Makhoba Omkhulu's daughter Ntombenhle who had begun to act strangely. If she was not avoiding me, she would snap at me over nothing. At first I dismissed her bad manners, blaming them on adolescent moodiness. A number of men had begun showing an interest in her. I attributed her peculiar attitude to the confusion experienced by most teenagers; she was probably preoccupied, thinking about her suitors. She was a few years older than me, a qhikiza, the oldest girl in the group who is seen as the leader; she was also the one whom suitors approached first before proposing to a girl in the group. I didn't feel comfortable confronting her about her behaviour and hoped that one day she would tell me whatever it was that was troubling her. That day came sooner than expected.

We were walking back from the river when she said quite casually, 'Tell me, Nombhosho, when are you people leaving?'

'Leaving? Where to? And why?' The questions shot out of my mouth as fast as if they were burning my tongue.

'When are you and your mother going to leave us?' she repeated herself as though she wanted to emphasise the question.

I didn't know what she was talking about.

'Why should we go anywhere? This is our home. Makhoba Omkhulu fetched us from the wilderness and brought us here. Why do you want us to go?'

She didn't answer me. We walked the rest of the way back home in silence. I was confused. I didn't understand how Ntombenhle, who was my sister, could want us to leave. My other cousins kept quiet, but I could see them directing surreptitious glances at me. These told me that they knew what Ntombenhle was talking about but they were not going to be involved.

When I got home, I found Mother busy making a grass mat. I put the calabash of water down and told her what Ntombenhle had said to me. Mother said nothing. She did not even look up from her work. It was as though I hadn't said anything. I didn't understand her reaction, and I wanted an explanation. My mind was in turmoil and I wasn't going to rest until I got an answer.

As I was wrestling with the many unanswered questions, including why Mother was not reacting, I thought I was perhaps being unrealistic in expecting Mother to know what Ntombi had meant. She was the one who owed me an explanation, not my mother. I decided that the right thing to do was to confront Ntombi. I also wanted MaNgubane to know what her daughter had said; maybe she could throw some light on the matter.

As I was getting ready to leave, Mother suddenly stopped working on her mat. It was as though she had read my mind. She raised her head, looked at me, and in her quiet manner asked: 'Where are you going?'

'I am going to talk to Ntombenhle; she needs to tell me why she wants us to leave,' I answered. 'I also want her mother to know about it.'

'Oh! Now you want to involve adults in your girlish pranks. Just do your chores,' Mother said, making it abundantly clear that she did not want to talk about the matter and that I should let sleeping dogs lie.

A few days later MaNgubane went past our hut. Mother was on her knees, cleaning the floor by smearing it with cow dung. We used dung for a number of things. It was dried and used as fuel; fresh dung was used as floor polish. Creative women could draw beautiful patterns on the floor. And fresh dung smelled good and healthy.

MaNgubane stopped outside our hut. With her hands on her hips she asked Mother: 'Hhawu, why are you busy fixing this little hut when you should be leaving? Or is it because you are expecting my husband to marry you? The sun will fall down and be picked on by the hens before that happens.' She clapped her hands loudly before walking away.

Mother did not answer her. She continued what she was doing. So that's what it was! Makhoba Omkhulu wanted to marry my mom. At last I had found the answer to my cousin's strange behaviour and utterances. Of late she and some of my other cousins had been avoiding me. Although their attitude made me suspicious that all was not right, I hadn't been able to put my finger on it. After MaNgubane's remark to my mother, things fell into place.

I started recalling incidents which had happened not too long ago. One afternoon I had gone to their hut hoping to spend the afternoon with my cousins. I knocked on the door but nobody opened for me. I kept knocking and asking whoever was inside to open for me, but nobody did. I could tell there were people inside the hut and I was baffled as to why they were not letting me in. I gave up and went back home. I had also noticed that lately Omkhulu's visits to our house were no longer as frequent as they used to be. My aunt's outburst explained everything.

We were not welcome here.

What puzzled me was, if we were not wanted here, where were we supposed to go? We had no other home except this one. I could not understand why my family was forsaking us. There was no point in asking Mother what was going on because I didn't think she had the energy to deal with the problem. We both suffered in silence.

I felt helpless. I wanted to fight to protect my mother but she would not let me. I wanted to tell Makhoba Omkhulu what his family was doing to us but I knew Mother would be angry with me if I did that. I could not talk to her about it or to my sister Ndumbutshu who was too young to understand what was happening. Yet she, too, was baffled by the estrangement. I bottled everything up and swore that I would somehow find a way of getting even with them.

After the incident with my aunt, life became even more difficult for us. I could tell that Makhoba Omkhulu was aware of the tension between the two families but chose not to do anything about it. I thought about his mother. Had she been around, Grandmother would have sorted out the situation with the minimum of fuss.

Now it was blatant hostility from Omkhulu's family. Occasionally Omkhulu would stop by to say hello, but he no longer stayed for even a small helping of mahewu. He continued to be pleasant and courteous to us, referring to my sister and me as 'izintombi zam', my girls, but this was now said from a distance and not with the warmth I was used to.

His wife and children no longer made any bones about the fact that we were not wanted at the homestead. We no longer received food from them. Gone were the days when we were sent a chunk of meat from Makhoba Omkhulu. He'd slaughter an animal and they would devour everything, and not give us even a small piece of intestine. The milk had also dried up. When I asked Mother why Omkhulu was not giving us milk any more, she just said, 'Did you bring back a cow from the cave?'

Mother did not complain about her treatment by my uncle and his wife. She quietly accepted the situation and carried on with her life. I very much wanted to ask Makhoba Omkhulu why he had searched for us when he knew that MaNgubane was not in favour of our returning. Hadn't he promised Ngebeza that he would look after us? What uncle abandons his nieces and his brother's widow like that? My father would never have done anything like that to any member of his family.

One afternoon my mother and I went to gather wood in the forest. The road to the forest went past MaNgubane's hut. She must have been watching us because on our way back she appeared just as we were about to pass her house. When I saw her my mouth went dry. I feared the worst. I could think of only one thing, that she was going to attack my mother. But I knew if she did that she would curse the day she was born because Mother would beat her severely. I knew Mother could hold her own. She could put the fighting sticks to good use. I had seen her in action when we were threatened by animals in the wild. I must confess that I silently wished that MaNgubane would start a fight to let Mother show her strength. I knew that Mother would give her a hiding that would put an end to her harassing us.

MaNgubane walked fast and caught up with us. She stopped almost in front my mother as if she meant to stop her from going past. With her hands on her hips, her favourite pose, she looked at my mother, taking her in with her eyes from top to toe. We sidestepped her and continued walking, ignoring her completely. But she quickly moved to stand in front of my mother once more and looked up at the bundle of wood on my mother's head.

Suddenly she clapped her hands, laughed and said, 'He–he! You are so popular, even snakes love you.'

My mother was accustomed to her sarcasm so she simply walked on as if nothing had been said. I thought my aunt had gone completely mad. We left her standing there and went on our way. When we got home we dropped our bundles of wood on the ground. To my horror a snake slithered out of my mother's bundle. She took a stick and killed it. And then she sat down and wept like a baby. I couldn't understand why she was so upset. This was not the first snake she had killed. When we were living on the mountain we had seen many snakes and she would simply get a stone or a stick and kill it. I couldn't fathom a reason for her reaction. When she stopped crying, she surprised me by saying that she would never forgive the white people for killing my father. Our misery was the result of the death of my father who had died at the white man's hands.

'I knew that your aunt did not like me but I did not realise until today how deep her hatred runs. What I cannot understand is why she hates me to the point where she would have been happy if I had been bitten by the snake.'

I felt a deep loathing for the white people who had killed my dad. I was also angry at the king for granting my father's request to go back into active service, allowing him to lead Mbilini's defeated battalion back to the battlefield. This regiment was annihilated at the battle of Hlobane.

I felt that the king had no business to continue the fight over the land that was so large it could be shared by all and I could not understand why he had been so stubborn in the face of adversity. He had lost many warriors and cattle as well as the land. What was he thinking? He should have given himself up and handed over to Somtseu the cattle that the man wanted. That way there would have been peace in the land. I recalled King Shaka's prophecy. 'You think by killing me you will rule the land? I can see the birds flying over the horizon. They will rule this land.'

Mother cried herself to sleep. When she woke up the next day, she told us we were leaving the homestead.

★

I could not sleep that night. My mind was in turmoil. I was tormented by what my sister had told me during the day about my grandmother and her mother's struggle through life. I could not understand how they could experience so much ill-luck. I was also perplexed by the nonchalant manner in which my sister Ahh viewed life. I looked at her lying on her bed across the room and admired her peaceful sleep, snoring softly like a cat purring, while I lay awake. I was thinking of pythons. She seemed peaceful and beautiful.

Sis Ahh was by no means a rich woman although she was definitely not poor. She survived on her hospital pension and what her children gave her. All her children had done well. They were living far away in various cities but they took good care of their widowed mother. She had everything she needed in the house, and all of it was functional, nothing fancy. There was no gate to her property, not because she couldn't afford to install one but because there was no need for security. She did not fear being attacked or robbed. She led a peaceful life surrounded by neighbours who were free to call on her at any time of night or day, asking her for all types of help from medical advice to financial assistance.

I found myself being envious of her life. I felt my township upbringing had disadvantaged me. It had alienated me from the things in life that matter. I was afraid of everything, from the sound of thunder and lightning to a mouse scratching on my outside door. Sis Ahh once said: 'You township people are a strange lot. You are afraid of cows and rainfall.' How true. For instance, motorists in Soweto have to be careful when driving around the location streets because township children play in them, oblivious of the cars going past, but let the rain fall and the streets will be empty.

Lying in bed I felt hollow. I resented the fact that I had been brought up in the townships. I couldn't help wondering what would have happened to me had I been raised in the rural areas where people had lived from time immemorial and everybody knew everybody. I began to understand why our father had often insisted on taking us on visits to our grandparents. It was his way of trying to keep us in touch with our culture and traditions. Would I have been different if I had grown up where the young people will tell you not only the name of the river where they get their water but also where the river starts and which ocean or river it flows into? A place where people respect the earth they walk on. Where people till the soil and patiently watch the plants grow, unlike some of us who think apples and tomatoes are grown at the supermarket. A place where there are no robbers, where homes do not have gates to keep intruders out, where there are no street lights to eclipse the beautiful stars in the sky. A place where traditional leaders hold a prominent position in the community and their word is law. Where local adults are revered and celebrated as purveyors of wisdom and history.

I had been raised in the townships where the white superintendent ruled the roost ensuring that the apartheid machinery was not only well oiled but was in motion. I grew up in places where my essence as an African was downplayed and my tribal affiliations trampled upon. Sometimes I would ponder on pronounce-

ments made by some suave township people as they made fun of what they regarded as country bumpkins. After the Tsonga people, it was the Zulus who suffered the worst township ridicule. Township 'clevers' often referred to uneducated Zulu people as 'Shaka se broer' – Shaka's brother. This comment was not meant as a compliment. It was meant to be a derogative description of a person who was not 'with it', what township people refer to as a 'moegoe', a 'square'. I now realised that the joke was on them because they obviously had no clue who Shaka was or the role he played in shaping the history of southern Africa.

I had grown up insulated, concerned only with survival in hostile townships and the cold city of Johannesburg. I missed out on the things that defined me as an African.

PART FOUR

Another Move

*M*y sister and I had made good progress with the writing of the book. I had also begun to understand quite a lot about Zulu culture and about the differences between the Amakholwa and the Amabhinca, that is, the Christians and the non-believers. Years back when I visited my parents in Zululand, I was often taken aback by the antagonism between the two groups, particularly by the Christians who at this time in history regarded themselves as a little bit superior to the non-believers since many were working in the mines and on the white-owned farms, while the non-Christians clung to the old traditions of eking out a living by tilling the earth. The Christians displayed contempt towards the non-believers. They openly despised almost everything about them. To make matters worse for the non-believers, their children did not attend school. This meant they could not read or write which put them at a disadvantage compared with church-going children. Of course I little knew that the Christian children were able to get an education because it was part of the religion package offered to them by the missionaries. However, it came at a huge 'national' price.

As my sister and I continued working on the book, I found myself wondering how she must have felt being left behind to live with Grandmother while the rest of us were in Venda. The reason my parents had given for not taking her with us was that the move would disrupt her schooling. They were to commence their ministry in Venda mid-year and she was to write her Junior Certificate exams at the end of the year so it made sense that she should stay behind and complete her studies. But I was curious as to how the separation had affected her.

I knew that the move to Venda had not been easy for my parents. They had many issues to deal with. First, they had to travel a long distance by train with small children on third-class tickets. Once in Venda, they had to learn the Venda language. They had to adapt to the local customs and traditions, and it took some time for the locals to warm to them because they were complete strangers from a different ethnic group. I recall Mother telling us that their worst fear while living in Venda was the prospect of having our eldest brother Stanford abducted and taken to an initiation camp to be circumcised. She said there were groups of bandits who prowled the villages at night looking for boys to take to the initiation camps. The idea of their son undergoing such a ritual was anathema to my parents because circumcision was not part of the Zulu culture. Fortunately the bandits never got hold of my brother.

Another fear which my parents harboured was the possibility of any of us dying from malaria while in Venda. Malaria was rife during those years. Many members of our church fell ill and died because hospitals were few and far between and medical science was not as advanced as it is now. I recall Father praying when we left Venda, thanking God that the family had been delivered from Venda intact. Those years, being posted to Venda was like going to another part of the world. Today Salvation Army officers – black and white – are sent to countries as far afield as Tanzania and Kenya, and officers from other parts of the continent have been posted to South Africa, something that was unheard of during the apartheid years.

'Weren't you resentful that you were left behind?' I asked Sis Ahh.

'In the beginning I was not upset that I had remained behind to be with Grandmother. Gogo was such a wonderful person. She told me that my parents had not taken me along because there were cannibals in Venda. It never occurred to me to ask her how come my parents were ready to expose my siblings to the *possibility of being devoured by the Venda cannibals. At the time I felt I was the chosen one, that my parents had opted to protect me of all their children. But as time went on, I began to miss all of you. I would sit and think of my little brothers and sisters and try to visualise what type of country Venda was. Sometimes I would get a letter from Father and I would read it over and over again. Did you know that he had a peculiar way of doing things? When he wrote a letter he would copy the same letter for himself and file it away. And he did not use a carbon paper. He literally copied the original letter word for word. He was just too organised. I think that must have been the church influence. But the best part was that, when I wrote back to him, he would post my reply back to me bleeding with corrections.' Sis Ahh laughed.*

She also said that living with Gogo was interesting because our mother was Gogo's first daughter and Sis Ahh her first grandchild, so she was treated like a queen. She had a special calabash for sour milk and she was the one who was privileged to collect the leftover food from Grandfather. In those days, elders did not eat everything on their plate. They left some food for their favourite child or grandchild. Today's youngsters would be scandalised by that practice.

'My grandparents often called me by my surname,' said Sis Ahh. 'Each time Gogo asked me to do something for her she would say "Please, Mntungwa" (the Khumalo clan praise name) and each time I did something well, like if I had done well at school, she would rattle off my family praise names.'

We continued working on the book. It was beginning to take shape. We had gone past the war ravages in Zululand and were now dealing with post-war problems. Our grandmother's voice seemed stronger than ever ...

★

Mother, my sister and I were once more on the road. The only difference was that this time we knew where we were going. Mother told us that we were going to Dundee to stay with her cousin MaMsweli. We were on the road for two days and two nights.

We arrived at the cousin's place on the morning of the third day and were met by MaMsweli's mother-in-law Khulu, who told us that MaMsweli had already gone to work in the fields and would be back around noon. Noting how tired and hungry we looked, she gave us a large calabash of mahewu, a drink of sour porridge, to quench our thirst and fill our bellies.

MaMsweli came back at midday. She was a big-busted, loud-voiced woman with an equally large personality. Her infectious laughter filled the entire hut. We took to her immediately and knew we would be safe with her. It was interesting to witness the joy the two women displayed at their reunion. They were cousins, their mothers were sisters, but the last time they had seen each other was at our mother's wedding when MaMsweli was part of the bridal entourage that had accompanied Mother to her new home with the Makhobas. Naturally the two women had a lot to talk about.

They recalled the war and how they had been affected by it. Mother told MaMsweli the reason for our visit. She began by narrating how Father had died in battle and how we had been left stranded on the mountain and later wandered all over Zululand, completely lost, until we were saved by the Ngebeza clan; how one day Makhoba Omkhulu came looking for us and took us back home with him and helped us reconstruct our lives.

Mother went on to tell MaMsweli how short-lived the happy reunion and good life with the Makhoba clan had been, because Makhoba Omkhulu decided to 'ngena' her. She related in detail how his wife MaNgubane and her children had reacted to this decision and how Makhoba Omkhulu, who in fact was responsible for the impasse, had opted to distance himself from us and the feud. Instead of allaying his wife's fears and telling her that my mother was not interested in the marriage, he had squirmed and avoided us. That was so cowardly, Mother told MaMsweli.

'It made no difference to MaNgubane that I was not interested in her husband,' Mother said. 'I made it abundantly clear to her and everyone else at the homestead that I did not want a husband. I was prepared to raise my children without a man. But of course the real reason was that MaNgubane had never liked me. It's no secret that our mother-in-law openly favoured me. I didn't tell anyone that we were leaving. Not even Makhoba Omkhulu. I feared that if I told him he would stop me from going, yet he was impotent. He could not protect me or my children against his wife. Since he was unable to do anything to remedy the situation, I simply took my children and left.'

MaMsweli clapped her hands and said in her booming voice, 'Yehheni! My sister, you disappoint me. You left your home because of a woman? You left because of someone of the same status as yourself? She is not a Makhoba. They paid lobola for her just as they did for you. Both you and MaNgubane know that ukungena is our custom. It was therefore a foregone conclusion that when Makhoba died one of his brothers should ngena you so that you and your children would be safe. My sister,' continued MaMsweli, 'it is our custom. It has nothing to do with love. It is about self-preservation. Look at you now. You are homeless. You criss-crossed the wilderness at risk of being devoured by wild animals, for what? You should have swallowed a stone, stayed and persevered for the benefit of your children. And as for MaNgubane, you should not have allowed her to intimidate you. Right now she is back there at the homestead and you are out in the cold.'

Then, changing the subject slightly, she said: 'My husband and yours suffered the same fate. Mine died earlier on at Rorke's Drift. I am on my own with my children and Khulu, who is my pillar of strength. I will talk to her and ask her if you and your children can stay with us. I don't think she will have any objection.'

The two women went back to talking about the war and its implications, lamenting how the white people had killed so many Zulu men as well as women and children.

'Look around you,' said MaMsweli. 'Do you see any men? They are all gone. Our brave heroes, the regiments of uSuthu, iNgobamakhosi, uThulwana, inDlondlo, uDhloko, uVe, umCijo, you name them, they are all gone. Dead and buried all over the plains and hills of Zululand.'

MaMsweli talked to Khulu about allowing us to live with them and she agreed. Later Khulu accompanied mother and MaMsweli to visit the induna for Mother to pay her respects and acquire the right to live in the village. We were granted permission to stay. Our new cousins, MaMsweli's children, were older than we were and they treated us like their younger siblings. They showed us around and made us comfortable. They took me with them to the river where we fetched water and went with me to the forest to fetch firewood.

Khulu took care of everybody at the homestead. She was the best grandmother after ours and, in effect, she became my grandmother. She was my favourite person in the homestead because she managed to close the hole that had been left by my granny's death.

In the beginning we shared MaMsweli's hut but it wasn't long before Khulu organised an ilima, as Makhoba Omkhulu had done on our arrival at his homestead, to assist us in building our huts. As host on this occasion, Khulu made sure that there was enough beer and meat to entertain the people who came to work. After the huts were built, the people had a feast, drinking beer and eating goat's meat. Khulu gave us a goat which I had to look after. We once more had a place called home and life seemed wonderful.

★

One day we heard that the king had returned to the nation. He came back the same way he had disappeared, unannounced. Just as the nation had not been informed when he was whisked away to wherever, there was no formal communication about his return. But the news of his sudden arrival was all over Zululand, reverberating on the mountains and in the valleys and sending shock waves throughout the region. Some people were ecstatic about his return while others were most unhappy.

The first person to break the news to us was MaMsweli. She knew about it because her aunt was one of King Cetshwayo's wives and the mother of Prince Dinuzulu, who at the time was about thirteen years old.

MaMsweli burst into the hut where Mother was on her knees grinding corn on the stone in preparation for supper. She walked in, panting and out of breath, not even pausing to greet my mother.

'Mzala, Cousin, the king is back,' she announced and began doing the indlamu, the Zulu dance, and chanting: 'Usuthu, Usuthu' while stamping her feet.

Mother pleaded with her to be calm and to tell her where she had heard the story, but MaMsweli continued dancing. Finally she walked away – I suppose to spread the news in the village.

For some days there was jubilation in the villages. Wherever one went, people talked about the return of the king. The ancestors had heard our prayers, they said. Although there were no formal festivities to welcome the king, his return was celebrated and people speculated that his return meant the demise of the reign of the kinglets who had been imposed on us by Shepstone's son, who we called Misjan. Some people travelled to Ondini to verify the news and to satisfy their curiosity. However, one particular story had tongues wagging. The king had come back dressed in white people's clothes. This bothered us, for it meant that the king had become a Christian and was therefore a deserter. The notion that he had capitulated to the foreigners was based on nothing but the fact that he no longer wore ibheshu, but wore invaders' clothes.

Five years after his disappearance and five years after the end of the war the king had returned transformed. Many of us were hurt about this. After all we had been through and suffered at the hands of the foreigners for supporting him, we could not understand how he could betray us and embrace the white people's ways. That was devastating. Whatever hopes we had that his return would reunite the nation and sort out the deserters were dashed, because we assumed that there was no way he could take up our cause now that he was one of them.

But it didn't take long for us to realise that the king was still the same person he had been before the war, even after suffering the loss of thousands of warriors and his land at the hands of the English. If anything, his abduction had afforded him direct exposure to the enemy, making him even more determined to fight for his land. We were also aware that the king faced not only white people as the enemy for there were now many Zulus who wanted him dead. Whereas his return should have been heralded as a blessing to the nation that had lamented his absence, it instead threw the Zulu people and the region into turmoil.

Soon after his return, an imbizo – a meeting – was called. Thousands of people travelled to Ondini to hear what the king had to say. Men, both young and old, traversed the plains and mountains from the many corners of Zululand, daring the wrath of Shepstone, who was definitely unhappy at the return of the king. Many wanted to see for themselves how the king had changed, so the paths to Ondini were crowded with curious subjects.

Under different circumstances, this imbizo would have been a joyous occasion, a celebration of victory over the enemy. King Cetshwayo had triumphed over the British – the fact that he was alive was in itself a victory. Instead, the meeting was marked with fear and trepidation. Misjan and his cohorts of onongqayi lurked in the background on the pretext that they were there to quell violence should any arise. There were the kinglets to contend with. They were worried about what was going to happen to them – were they going to be demoted and become common people, or what? As for the deserters, they seemed ambiguous about their future – they didn't know whether to dump their white masters and go back to the king or stay on with the white people. Then there were the white settlers who spewed all types of vitriol against the king.

By daybreak uZulu had converged at the palace. The energy emanating from the waiting crowds chanting war songs was electrifying and further enhanced by the intermittent thunder of drums accompanied by the melancholic wail of muted horns. Around noon, the drums stopped and a hush fell as the voice of the praise singer burst on the scene, announcing the appearance of King Cetshwayo:

uJininindi omnyama – the very dark general
ongabubende bezingwe nobezingonyama – dark as the blood of the leopard
ohlathi limnyama, limnyama konke nemizi yalo – the dark forest and its
environs
ibululu lika Phunga noMageba – Phunga and Mageba's python
Elidond'ukusuka kwaze kwasuk'awezindlwana – who is slow to act

Here the praise singer was using the colour black and the depiction of a snake as a metaphor to depict power. The king walked slowly into the arena. He was indeed dressed in foreigners' clothes. The only item that remained to denote his tradition and his status was isicoco – the black rubber-like head ring. Otherwise everything about his appearance was alien. After the praise singer had concluded his performance, the king sat down and as he did so, the meeting place was suddenly engulfed by a frightening silence. Although this eerie feeling lasted less than two seconds, it seemed like an eternity.

Then as if someone was conducting a choir, the regiments – the iNgobamakhosi, uVe, uFalaza and some veterans from iSangqu, uThulwana, uNokhenke and many other war survivors – saluted the king in unison: 'Bayede, wena wendlovu', Hail to the king.

The king was not a garrulous and long-winded person. He greeted his subjects and reassured them that he was still their king and would lead the nation till his dying day. He told them he had been abducted and taken to Cape Town and later to England where he was paraded before the British Queen. He spoke, merely relaying the facts. When he had finished talking he stood up and once more the praise singer began chanting his praises before the king disappeared into his hut and the crowds dispersed.

Many people were unsurprised that the king had not touched on the developments that had taken place in his absence. They knew that he held discussions of that nature at the palace with his indunas and not with the rank and file. We knew that the king faced many problems, the most pressing of which was how he was to recoup his land and authority because Somtseu had divided Zululand into thirteen regions and installed kinglets to oversee these areas. These kinglets, who the invaders referred to as chiefs, had no powers. Power resided with the English. The chiefs were merely caretakers for the British throne. But even though they did not have power to govern they enjoyed huge privileges that came with their positions as caretakers. These included receiving a stipend from the English government and control of the distribution of land among the inhabitants. Naturally, as custodians, they were in a position to apportion themselves huge chunks of land.

Two of the thirteen kinglets Somtseu had installed were Hhamu and Zibhebhu. Hhamu was the king's uncle who, during the war between Dingane and the Boers, had defected to the Boers in the Transvaal taking a whole regiment with him and leaving Dingane in the lurch. He returned after King Dingane had been defeated.

Zibhebhu, another uncle, was a skilful fighter and had been one of the king's generals during the Anglo-Zulu war. During the king's absence, Zibhebhu had been installed as a chief and allocated the Usuthu region, which was King Cetshwayo's stronghold. He secretly harboured grandiose ideas of becoming the king of Zululand, seeing himself as the natural successor to King Cetshwayo.

Last but not least, the king's erstwhile friend Jantoni, that is John Dunn, who during the war had turned his back on the Zulu people and fought on the side of the English, had been installed as a kinglet and allotted a large area to govern. He had accepted this position on the supposition that the king would never return to Zululand.

After the king's return, the first to revolt were the kinglets who saw this as the end to their authority and privileges. Of all the king's adversaries, there were none as loathsome and dangerous as the unholy trio, Hhamu, Zibhebhu and Jantoni.

In no time, Zululand was plunged into a series of severe battles. The worst was between the king and his uncle Zibhebhu. The king suffered a huge trouncing and lost to Zibhebhu. Many of his regiments were killed in that battle. Soon afterwards the king was reported to be ill and he died – he probably died of heartache, but rumour had it that he was poisoned. His son Dinuzulu was installed as the king of the Zulu people.

We did not shed tears when the king died. There were none left to shed. Our eyes had dried out after years of weeping for the many regiments that had perished trying to save the land. They had dried out after years of agonising about the king's disappearance. They had dried out after crying over the loss of our loved ones. They had dried out lamenting the cracks that divided the nation. Instead of screaming and wailing at the top of our voices, we silently mourned the child of Mpande, the lion of Ondini.

The king was dead and the nation died with him. We were left with the hope that his ancestors were ready to receive him and give him back his isicoco for the gallant way in which he had defended his people. The uThulwana, umKhulutshane, umCijo, uDududu, iSangqu and uVe regiments were waiting to welcome him.

★

Life went on in the villages and at our homestead. Then one day Khulu called Mother to her hut.

'Mtanami, my child, I have called you because I have something to tell you. Life has become increasingly difficult for all of us and I can no longer afford to have you living here. For one thing, I need to have my fields back. However, I am not throwing you to the dogs. I know someone who is in need of a wife. I have decided that you must accept his proposal so that you have somewhere to live.'

'What if I don't want to marry him?'

'Then you will have to find your own place to stay,' said Khulu.

She told Mother that the man she had in mind worked for a farmer in Dundee, and lived on that farm. She said she believed he was a good man. His wife had died during the war, and he was looking for someone to help him raise his children.

For weeks Mother went about with a sad face. She had the look that she often wore at the Makhoba household shortly before we left. It pained me to see my mother looking miserable and not knowing the cause of her anguish. I did not have to wait long to hear the reason. One evening she sat us down and told my sister and me about the man who wanted to marry her, and that she was considering accepting his proposal.

'A woman needs a man to protect her in this world,' she said. 'People undermine and abuse unprotected women.'

'This doesn't make sense to me,' I told her. 'MaMsweli does not have a husband, why isn't Khulu organising one for her?'

'She has to look after Khulu, that's why. There is no reason for Khulu to let her go and none for MaMsweli to leave her. After all, she is the widow of Khulu's son, and MaMsweli's children are Khulu's own grandchildren,' was Mother's reply.

After that revelation I was confused and sad for many days. I didn't know how this marriage would affect us. If Mother wanted to get married, why had she declined marriage to Makhoba Omkhulu? He would have offered us better security than a stranger and moreover we would still have been a family. I couldn't follow her reasoning. I did however have to admit to myself that with MaNgubane present our chances of being accepted by the family were slim.

Soon thereafter Mother told us that she was definitely going to marry the stranger and that he would be visiting one of these days.

The man arrived one sunny morning at a homestead that was bustling with activity. Everyone was very excited and had prepared a big feast. MaMsweli and my mother had made sorghum beer, slaughtered a number of chickens and cooked corn bread and amadumbe, a popular Zulu vegetable which is a cross between a potato and yam.

He arrived in style, on horseback, looking immaculate in his brown baggy trousers and an army-type jacket. With the brim of his hat cocked to the left so that it almost covered his left eye, he reined in the horse and slowly dismounted. By then, the entire household was out to welcome the man from town. I was more curious about him as the man who was to marry my mother. I watched him dismount and I felt like screaming. He looked ancient. I took an immediate dislike to him. I could not imagine a man who looked as old as my grandfather taking my father's place. I couldn't help remembering my father, how handsome, tall and strong he had been. This man was thin, grey, slightly stooped, and occasionally flashed a smile that revealed numerous missing teeth. I was bewildered that Mother could have agreed to marry such a man.

The man came well prepared. He sat down and we proceeded with the usual pleasantries and the introductions. When my mother later called me and Ndumbutshu to meet the man, whose name we were told was Mbuyisa, he coyly opened a sack full of gifts. He gave mother beautiful mabhayi to wear over her shoulders. Ndumbutshu and I also received presents of colourful mabhayi and beads.

In spite of the spirit of conviviality that pervaded our homestead that afternoon, our guest of honour seemed ill at ease and appeared more nervous than my mother. I think this may have been because he didn't quite know where he stood with my mother. Little did we know then how well Khulu had cleared the way for him; we later learned that he was Khulu's brother.

This was supposed to be a happy day for all of us and I seemed to be the only one who did not enjoy the festivities. I was miserable. Despite the slight awkwardness accompanying a first meeting, it was a fait accompli that Mother would marry Mbuyisa.

Indeed, no time was wasted. Soon after Mbuyisa's visit, Mother told my sister and me that we would be leaving shortly to join him at the farm. I had no idea what life on a farm was like. Of course I had seen white people's homesteads, which were referred to as farms, but I had no clue what went on at such places.

The old man came back for us a few days later. We were once more separated from people we loved. We left Khulu, my ever-cheerful Aunt MaMsweli and my cousins. It was another sad day in my life.

Once more we were on the move. The difference was that this time we did not have to walk. The old man came to fetch us driving a sleigh pulled by oxen. The four of us were crammed in the small confines of the sleigh with bundles of our belongings, such as grass mats and blankets, cooking utensils, calabashes of sour milk and clothing. We were on the road for almost two days, eventually arriving at the farm at midnight. Mbuyisa ushered us into a strange-looking hut. It wasn't round like our huts, it was big and square without grass roofing. My sister and I were shown where we were to sleep. We unfolded our grass mats and took our blankets and made our beds. I was so tired from the journey that I fell asleep at once.

PART FIVE

The Farm

I woke up to see light filtering into the room. I was scared when I found that the man's hut had a hole in the wall that let in the sunlight because it meant that ghosts, witches and all the other night creatures must have had a field day watching us whilst we slept. I woke my little sister up. She too was shocked at the light coming into the hut. When Mother came to wake us up, she found us already wide awake and huddled together in the corner like we used to do in the caves when we were scared. I learned later that the hole that let the light into the hut was called a window and all the houses in that area were fitted with windows.

Mbuyisa came in carrying tin mugs of tea and a plate of cornbread slices smeared with jam. He asked if we had slept well and then told us to eat and get ready to meet Oubaas, the owner of the farm, to pay our respects. I watched him as he handed us the food. He had soft kind eyes and he seemed to care about us genuinely. Maybe I had been wrong about him. Maybe he was old but he was kind. Maybe, just maybe, by marrying him, Mother had made the right decision. I decided to give him a chance.

After breakfast, we were taken to Oubaas. As I walked out of the house, my eyes fell on a huge building half a mile away. Built on top of a hill and overlooking the river, the breathtaking structure looked like a cliff. I had never seen such a settlement before. Even the wealthy induna who had been in charge of our village before the war did not have half the number of huts that were on this property. The induna, who had been the envy of many people in the village, had had many huts and rondavels built of mud and grass. I stood in awe, looking at this edifice. I could not figure out the type of material that could support such high walls. Seeing wonderment written all over my face, Mbuyisa pointed to the place and said: 'That is Oubaas's property. That's where he lives with his family.'

'Who is Oubaas? Is he the induna?' I asked.

The old man laughed and told me that Oubaas was the owner of the property I was looking at, and that he also owned the place where we had spent the night. The road leading to the property was flanked by huge wattle trees. The main building was an imposing white-painted brick house with small huts and water tanks alongside it. There was a broad cobbled road which led to a cattle kraal housing over two hundred cattle and another huge pen housing about a thousand sheep. Next to it was a pig sty which faced the stables. We walked towards the house where we were to meet Oubaas.

It was a truly enormous building with doors and windows all around it. As we approached the house we were confronted by a long veranda with a shining black floor. While I was quietly taking in the wonderment of this building, I saw something that looked like an apparition on the veranda. On taking a closer look, I realised it was not a ghost I was seeing, but some strange-looking human being. I held my mother's hand even more tightly. By then we were very close to the veranda and I could see what was sitting on the stoep was, without a doubt, not human. I heard Mbuyisa whisper to Mother, 'That is Oubaas.'

I didn't know what to think. For weeks I had been preoccupied with the thought of my mother marrying the old man. I had not for a moment thought about what lay ahead for us, such as who owned the farm? What we were going to do once we got there? I suddenly realised that I was now a 'deserter'; I was about to be owned by the enemy. As I got closer to what I still took to be an apparition, I remembered what my father had said when we were in the caves, when he cautioned me, telling me not to wish to meet white people. At the time, I had heard so much about white people and their powerful artillery that I would have paid any price to see what they looked like.

Oubaas continued sitting on the chair on the stoep smoking his pipe and reading a newspaper even as we got close to him. Mbuyisa stopped when we were a few paces away. As for me, I was gazing at a replica of a human being. I had never seen anything like him before. He had a strange colour as though drained of blood. Where there was supposed to be hair, I saw something like sisal plant strands hanging down from his head to his neck. I was convinced I was looking at a ghost and this was happening in broad daylight. I was so scared I couldn't bring myself to continue looking at him.

I had seen many wild animals such as monkeys and baboons that resembled humans but I had never seen anything that was supposed to be a person and yet did not look like me. What had gone wrong, I wondered. I caught a glimpse of the skin on his arms. It was not like the skin of any person I knew. It seemed rough and dry and I could see the green veins and some black marks on his arms. We were now so close to him that we were almost face to face. At that point he dropped the newspaper on the floor, raised his face and looked at us. I almost fainted.

143

His eyes were green like a mamba's and his nose was long and sharp as though it had been chiselled.

Old man Mbuyisa took his hat off and greeted his master.

'Sawubona, mnumzane.' Good day, sir.

Responding in impeccable isiZulu, Oubaas greeted the old man and said, 'I see you are back. Now which one is your wife?'

Pointing to my mother, Mbuyisa answered: 'This one is and these are her children.'

'Good,' said Oubaas. 'She will have to join the workers in the fields and this one,' pointing at me, 'will look after my children. You will have to buy them clothes to wear. I will not have naked kaffirs on my property.'

With these words he signalled with his hands that he was through talking to us. Mother was in her black pleated hide skirt and a new ibhayi which the old man had bought her. It covered the rest of her body. My sister and I were wearing the tiny bead skirts covering our private parts and the rest of my body was covered in my ibhayi. Around my neck was a string of beads that not only adorned my torso but made a feeble attempt at covering my chest which boasted breasts that were the size of tennis balls and proudly stood at attention. I was now a full-blown teenager, and my body was in bloom. Having taken after my father, I was tall and fair of complexion. My arms were strong and my thighs were round and full. I was a picture of health.

The old man took his cue to depart and decided to take us to the shop to get some clothes. On the way, I asked him, 'What does the word "kaffir" mean?'

'Oh, that is a word whites use to refer to us.'

'Why does he call us that? Doesn't he know we are Zulus?' I asked.

Mbuyisa did not answer me. I decided not to press him further for an explanation. I didn't want him to think I was being insolent.

We walked to the shop that was located on the border of the farm and next to the main road to the town. It was a huge brick structure with a long veranda that had an assortment of merchandise on it. We picked our way into the shop avoiding bumping against bicycles hanging from the rafters, sheets of dried cowhide, wheelbarrows and all types of farming tools, as well as numerous bags of mealies waiting to be ground on the milling machine. Boxes were filled with different kinds of vegetables.

The inside of the shop was divided into many sections. There was a food section with items such as bags of mealie meal, sugar, dry beans, samp and bottles of oil. The next counter dealt with utility merchandise such as paraffin stoves, water cans and enamel utensils like mugs and plates. Another corner of the shop housed bales and bales of cloth. The shelves next to them had everything to do with sewing, from sewing needles to buttons and scissors.

The shop was full of customers. The old man looked around and then led us to a man who was standing at one of the counters. He told us the man owned the shop. He looked exactly like Oubaas. He, too, had a dry lifeless skin and strands of something hanging down from his head. Another apparition!

'What is wrong with these people?' I asked my mother. 'Why are they the way they are? Are they normal people?'

'Yes, they are normal people, just like us,' said Mother. 'The only difference is that they are white and they are not good people.'

Mbuyisa was quick to say, 'They are neither good nor bad. They are different from us. You will get to know them.' He introduced Mother to the shop owner.

'Nkosana, this is my wife and these are her children.'

The trader burst out laughing. I thought he was laughing at the old man for addressing him as nkosana. What was a nkosana? Was it something like him? Were such people called nkosanas? The word means 'small king'. There was no big or small king in my country; one was either a king or a commoner. I then recalled that the first time I heard the word 'nkosana' was from a deserter and she was referring to her master.

'You must be joking. What is an old man like you doing with a young woman like her? The local dogs will show you a thing or two, I tell you. Don't say I didn't warn you,' the man said in impeccable Zulu and then changed from making personal remarks to talking business. 'What can I get you?'

'I want to buy material to make dresses for my wife and the children. Please add the amount to my account for the month-end.'

Mother was told to choose the cloth she liked from the stack of bales against the wall and the shop owner called his wife. Yet another apparition! What was I expecting? She looked just like Oubaas and the trader. She was a tiny woman with grey hair, mean eyes and pinched lips as though she seldom opened her mouth. Her husband told her that she must make dresses for us.

The woman took out her measuring tape, motioned to us to come closer and got down to business. I noticed that she did not ask us what type of dresses we wanted. Nor did she once address us. She wore a perpetual frown on her face and her nose wrinkled as though she was struggling to look at something she didn't fancy or that smelled foul. She busied herself taking our measurements. Without saying a word to us, she simply put the measuring tape where she needed it to be, and wrote down the measurements. With her index finger she would indicate to whoever she was measuring at the time that she should turn around. I thought maybe she could not speak. Once the job was done, she turned and said, 'Next Friday,' and disappeared to her sewing room.

We walked back to the farm and found Oubaas seated at the same spot where we had left him earlier. Mbuyisa reported to him that he had organised clothes for us but that they would only be ready in a week's time. He asked Oubaas if it would be all right if we started work once we had our clothes.

Oubaas looked at the old man with a sneer on his face and said: 'In the meantime, what will these people be doing on my property? They will be eating and shitting on my property for free?'

I saw my mother cringe and I knew then her marrying the old man had been a big mistake. Once more my father's words flashed through my mind. *'You must pray never to see a white person for as long as you live.'* However, that day had come and it was clear to me no good would come out of our stay at the farm. I now understood why the king had fought tooth and nail to stop these people from settling in our land.

While we were standing there not knowing whether to go back to where we had slept or wait for our marching orders, Oubaas called out for his wife Nona. A fat woman emerged from the kitchen. This time I wasn't taken aback. I was only surprised to see how tall and fat she was. There were no fat people in those years. The last time I saw a fat woman was before we went to live in the mountains. Nona asked Oubaas who we were and what the problem was. When her husband told her we were the new recruits to the farm she immediately allotted us our places of service. She turned and looked at me as she spoke to her husband.

'You say she will be able to look after the children. This will relieve Khosi who will now work full-time in the kitchen. This is good news. Are they to start now?'

'Yes,' answered Oubaas.

I was taken to the kitchen where I was introduced to her three small children. Oubaas, Nona and the children seemed to be cut from the same cloth. The children were fat like their mother and they looked me up and down curiously. I was scared of them, with their straight loose hair and green eyes. I could not imagine living with these creatures. How would I possibly look at those eyes?

'Ntombazana, what is your name?' asked Nona.

'My name is Nombhosho but everybody calls me Mbhosho.'

'Oh, I think I will just call you Ntombazana. These are the children that you will be looking after. I don't want to hear my children cry. They are wonderful children. They are not fretful. You must make sure that you keep them happy, otherwise Oubaas and I will teach you a lesson. I must warn you that they will tell me if you beat them; besides, unlike you people with skins like an elephant, my children bruise easily. I will catch you out if you so much as pinch them,' she said as she walked away from me.

She was formidable. I didn't know which of the two – Oubaas or his wife – was more frightening. My mind was reeling with fear. Although I had been in numerous situations where I had been scared out of my wits, standing before this couple was yet another terrifying moment in my life. Where would it end?

I was introduced to Khosi, one of Mbuyisa's daughters, who took me to a two-bedroomed hut which she shared with three other girls. The hut was huge and similar to the one the old man lived in. She told me that the two girls sharing her room also worked in the kitchen and there were six others who worked in the fields sharing the other bedroom.

'Why don't you live with your father in his hut?' I asked. 'Do you prefer it here?'

'It's not what I prefer. We are not allowed to stay with our parents, so that Oubaas and Nona can keep an eye on us. You too will be sleeping here.'

She showed me the room where I would be sleeping. It had grass mats hanging on the wall and blankets piled in a corner. Next to the blankets were some buckets. Khosi noticed that I was curious about the buckets.

'Oh, you want to know about these?' she said pointing at the buckets. 'Before we go to sleep, we have to fill them with water and place them next to our grass mats. If one oversleeps, Oubaas will come and kick over the bucket and the person who slept beyond the waking hour will be soaked in water. Oubaas will then hit that person with the sjambok.'

After showing me where I would be sleeping, she gave me one of her old dresses to wear. As I had never worn a dress before, I didn't know how to start putting it on. She showed me how it was to be worn. It was my size, but it was long and I felt strange in it, as if I would trip and fall each time I took a step. After I had put on the dress, Khosi took me back to the main house and found Nona in the kitchen.

'Khosi,' she said, 'I want you to spend this week showing Ntombazana how I want my children looked after. Show her how to give them a bath and how I want them fed. I don't ever want to hear my children complain, you understand. My babies will tell me if you dare treat them badly and you will be sorry.' She looked at me sternly.

In the evening we received our food rations and were joined by the girls who worked in the fields. While we ate our supper, the girls introduced me to life on the farm. They told me that Oubaas in particular and his wife, to a lesser degree, were notorious in the neighbourhood for ill-treating their servants. They said, 'Even the local farmers dislike Oubaas for the manner in which he treats his workers.' They advised me never to make him angry.

'He will hang you from a tree and lynch you,' one of the girls said. 'We've seen him do that to a boy who lost a sheep. He beat the boy and left him for dead. Oubaas did not seem to care.'

That night, for the first time in my life, I was parted from Mother and Ndumbutshu. This was the beginning of a new life for me. With the umbilical cord snapped, I didn't know if I would survive in this household. In all our travails and suffering, Mother had been at my side. There was never a time when she had left us on our own. Now I had to grope around this strange terrain without my compass. That thought was terrifying.

★

I gradually acclimatised to life on the farm. Our days started at the crack of dawn. I worked in the kitchen helping Khosi with the preparation of breakfast. Once the children were up, I fed them and ensured that they were all right. I spent my days in the company of the toddlers, and if they were asleep, I helped in the kitchen. I spent the evenings with Khosi and the other girls. It didn't take me long to accept that I had been wrenched from my mother and was now living with my peers. We had a lot in common. Some of the girls were orphans, their parents victims of the war.

Soon my dress arrived. Even though I didn't really know anything about white people's clothes, I could tell that it was a bad job. The dress was far too big and completely shapeless. The other girls laughed at me when I tried it on and suggested I should use my beads as a belt to give it shape. A part of me did not care to give it shape because that would mean acceptance of my new status. With the dress, the transformation from an independent traditional Zulu girl to a slave was now complete. My identity was gone; I was no longer Makhoba's girl. From now on I would be referred to as Oubaas's girl. I was not permitted to go and see my mother; I was told I could visit her only on my day off which was one Sunday a month.

My work schedule was easy. In the mornings I went to the main house and prepared the children's breakfast. After they had eaten, I took them out to the playground. Contrary to my fears about the children giving me a hard time, I was surprised to find that they liked me, especially the oldest boy, Kleinbaas. All he wanted to do was eat and play. He liked playing hide-and-seek and getting under my skirt. It took me some time to get used to their appearance. At first I was afraid to touch them, but soon I was able to clean them up without noticing that they were different from me.

During the day when the children had their nap, I helped in the kitchen where there was always something to be done. Nona was meticulous about her kitchen. She was orderly, demanding that each item be in its place and she screamed at us when she couldn't find what she was looking for. At times she'd indiscriminately slap anyone next to her when this happened. 'It's supposed to be here. Where is it?' she shouted.

Gradually the kitchen girls initiated me into some of the domestic chores. They taught me how to scrub the floors, how to peel potatoes and how to clean the rooms. I learned quickly and it didn't take long for them to show me how to cook. They showed me how to prepare roasts and knead the dough to make bread. I was also shown how to make cheese and how to carve meat and spice it to be served cold. I was taught how to make brawn, a concoction of various pieces of pork cooked together with the trotters and left to cool. It turned into a slab of cold meat.

There was a lot of food in the house. I can still smell the strong aroma coming out of the pantry and the kitchen. In the beginning I could not stand the smell of onions and the various herbs and spices that were used in preparing the food. I was introduced to foodstuffs like bread and potatoes. It took me some time to acquire a taste for the food that was cooked and eaten at the farm. I'll never forget the first time I tasted bread. It was awful. I tried to chew on a piece of this dry stuff and it kept rolling and rolling around my mouth. But once I got used to the taste and the feel of it, I began enjoying it and even became the best bread maker on the farm. Nona soon noticed this and assigned me to be the one to knead and make bread for her family. The other girls were left to make bread for the farm workers. The one thing I never got used to eating was fish. To me, fish resembled a snake and I couldn't possibly eat a snake.

There was a surfeit of milk on the farm and many calabashes filled with sour milk. We prepared food not only for the family but also for the farm manager and his family who took their meals with Oubaas and Nona. The farm workers were given rations of mealies, milk and vegetables and when Oubaas slaughtered an animal, he would give the workers meat.

It didn't take me long to realise that Nona was not such a bad person nor was she so different from us. Although she had a temper and snapped at us when we made mistakes, most of the time she was fun to be around. Sometimes she even complained to us about Oubaas's shortcomings. We shared jokes with her and she taught us a lot. She was generous with food, allowing us to eat anything from her kitchen and she encouraged us to learn to cook.

'What will you give your husband and children to eat if you cannot cook?' she would say to us. 'Come, let me show you how to prepare this dish.'

A woman who had been a worker on the farm had managed to marry someone living in the village, although I could not grasp how this had happened. Occasionally this woman's daughter visited the farm. Whenever she arrived we would inform Nona who would invite her in. The child had to remove her shoes before entering the house.

'Oh! You are grown up now. What do you learn at school? Can you speak English for us?'

'Yebo, Nona,' answered the little girl.

'Can you say a few words of English?'

The girl would say something in English and an impressed Nona would say: 'You really sound like English people. Here you are, take this piece of meat for your mom.'

One day I was tidying Nona's bedroom when I suddenly saw a girl doing exactly what I was doing. I looked at this person and she stared back at me. I knelt on the floor and she also went down on her knees. I knew I was in trouble. If the person stole something from the room it was I who was going to be blamed.

I went looking for Khosi in the kitchen and told her what I had seen. She suggested that we go back to the bedroom. This time there were two strange people in the room, although the other person looked a great deal like Khosi. I nudged her and pointed out the two strangers. To my surprise, Khosi burst out laughing uncontrollably. Tears streamed down her cheeks. Nona came charging from the living room.

'What's going on?' she asked.

'Nkosazana, Ntombazana saw her image in the mirror and she thinks there is a stranger in the house,' Khosi answered her and laughed again. And so did Nona. For days they looked at me, exchanged glances and laughed. Of course I had seen my reflection occasionally in a pond but that was quite different and was easily obliterated. I had never seen a mirror before.

We started work before dawn and only got back to our huts late at night. I seldom saw my mother and my little sister. I got along well with the girls, particularly the ones working in the kitchen. They reminded me of my cousins.

If living in the caves in the mountains had been difficult, living at the farm was hell of a different kind. I spent many nights lying awake, wondering why Mother had agreed to come and live with the old man. Wouldn't it have been better if she had married Makhoba Omkhulu? I did realise that, without a doubt, we would have lived as part of the

Makhoba clan, and could not understand what Mother gained by getting married to Mbuyisa and joining him in this hellhole.

On one of the rare days when I visited my mother we began talking about farm life. I asked her why she had opted to marry Mbuyisa. 'You knew the old man was a farm worker which means you knew he was working for white people. Father died trying to stop these very people from usurping our land and turning us into slaves, and yet you married him. Why, why Mother, why?'

'I had hoped to explain this to you when you were older but, since you ask, I will tell you now.'

Mother told me that Khulu had given her an ultimatum: she should marry the old man or else leave her property. 'When I refused to marry her brother she told me to leave her homestead. She explained that not only could she no longer support us, but also that her brother had offered a token lobola for me which she, Khulu, could not afford to turn down. She also needed the fields that we were utilising. I had nowhere to go. I couldn't go back to the Makhobas because I had left the family under a cloud and without warning. There was only one thing I could do: go with the old man.'

'Did your cousin MaMsweli go along with this?' I asked her.

'Her hands were tied. There was nothing she could do because her mother-in-law had made up her mind.'

I didn't know what to think. I could not believe that the woman whom I thought to be an angel was not only devious but ready to sacrifice anyone to achieve her ends. Again I realised that the world was full of evil and deceitful people, and there was no running away from them. First, it was the invaders who had killed and driven us off our land. Then it was my uncle who wanted to step into my father's shoes and when that did not happen he turned his back on us – and this after he had promised Ngebeza that he would look after us. Then there was Omkhulu's wife, MaNgubane, who hated my mother with such a passion that she made sure Mother and her own nieces were driven away for good. Now there was Khulu who had pretended she was offering mother a lifeline when she was in actual fact sending her to what she must have known was hell on earth. As for my aunt MaMsweli, she had washed her hands of us to protect her own interests. Yet in these times of unrest and uncertainty, who could blame her?

★

Oubaas ran the farm with an iron fist and everyone, including some of the neighbouring farm owners, was in awe of him. He was unpredictable and one often did not know what had sparked his anger. And when he was angry, he would strike out at anyone near him. He often shouted at his wife and when that happened we made sure that we got out of the way and hid in the pantry.

Work on the farm was not too bad. There were many hands to share the load and we worked harmoniously in the kitchen, and I loved playing with the children. In the evenings we gathered in one room with the girls who worked in the fields, shared a meal and told stories. We all had stories to tell, and the one thing our stories had in common was that they were all sad recollections of our lives.

For instance, my stepsister Khosi's mother had died during the war giving birth. The children were left destitute until a neighbour took them in. When her father came back from the war he found his home had been burnt down by the Redcoats and his animals confiscated. He was so devastated that he did not have the energy to start life afresh. He thanked his neighbours for taking care of his children after the death of their mother, took his two girls and came to the farm looking for work. He knew that he was no longer young and strong, but his girls were, and they were going to be the passport to all of them finding work and shelter. Oubaas took him in and made him look after the cattle, the older girl Ubukwani was sent to work in the fields and Khosi was to work in the kitchen. The other girls in the room were orphans. Oubaas had bought them from a farmer who claimed he had found them roaming aimlessly on his property sometime during the war.

There were about six families living and working on Oubaas's farm. Some of them had sons who also worked on the farm. These boys and men were not allowed to fraternise with us. Woe unto any man who was caught with so much as a foot in our yard! Oubaas would strap him to the trunk of a tree and whip him until he bled.

At times, particularly over weekends, we changed into our tribal garb and visited girls from the neighbouring farms. We might even attend a wedding in the neighbourhood. There we would sing and dance and drink beer. Sometimes the fun made us so nostalgic that we ended up weeping, thinking about the good old days when we were free.

Oubaas did not mind us wearing our traditional clothing as long as we did not do so in the main house. Sometimes we passed him on the road, riding uGagasi – the wave – his white horse. It was named uGagasi because, like the ocean wave, it carried Oubaas up and down the valley. Sometimes he was seen at odd places which were frequented by the local girls. Nobody dared question his presence at such places because he was the lord of the manor.

Although I was still young and not quite conversant with matters sexual, I knew that Oubaas was doing something bad with one of the girls who worked in the fields. I had been reliably informed by Khosi that Hlakazeka, the girl in question, had been chased away from working in the kitchen by Nona. Oubaas had then told her to join the workers in the field. He, together with the manager, handled the field workers. The problem was that during the winter months there was not much work for them and Hlakazeka and her paramour had plenty of time to themselves.

One evening I was delayed in the kitchen because Nona was sick and could not tuck the baby in. When I left the main house I was under the impression that Oubaas was in the living room. It was dark outside as I ran towards our hut. As I approached it, I saw movements of what I thought were human figures at the corner of the veranda. I froze. I could not imagine anybody brave enough to want to be in our yard at that hour. The first thing that came to my mind was that should Oubaas catch them, he would kill them. I feared it might be Fahlaza, a young farm worker who had a thing going with one of the farm girls. I knew that he was naughty but I didn't think he would be so stupid as to venture into our quarters. After a few minutes I gathered my strength and walked towards my room.

Unfortunately I had to go past the strange people. As I stepped onto the veranda my eyes fell on a big hat. I knew immediately who the hat belonged to. It was Oubaas's hat. I pretended not to notice anything as I picked up my pace, opened the door to my room and collapsed on the floor.

I was happy to find Khosi already asleep; I did not have to explain why I was so out of breath. I unrolled my grass mat, took my blankets, lay down and tried to fall asleep, but I could not erase from my mind what I had seen on the veranda. I was old enough to know what was going on and it didn't make sense to me. There were many stories told about how Oubaas fancied African girls. How could he, who treated us worse than dirt, be having a sexual liaison with Hlakazeka? But it confirmed the rumours I had heard about both of them. I had often defended Hlakazeka thinking that people were spreading malicious rumours about her simply because they were jealous of her. She was strikingly beautiful and she flaunted it. She was tall with a firm body. Her dark skin was flawless. Her broad lips encased a set of even white teeth and she had big sleepy eyes. She had a carefree personality and was at home in any company. She sang while she worked in the fields and often teased the male workers who treated her with kid gloves because, I assume, they knew that she had a thing going with Oubaas.

I didn't say anything to anyone about what I had seen the night before, nor did I ever mention it to anyone during the days that followed. For months I harboured the secret of what I had seen on the veranda, while inwardly I feared what the outcome of this liaison might be.

That day arrived sooner than I had anticipated. One warm summer's night, Hlakazeka gave birth to a baby girl. In the morning word of the tiny new arrival was mentioned to Nona. On receiving the news, Nona stormed into our hut demanding to see mother and baby. The first thing she said when she saw the baby was: 'Who is the father of this baby?'

Hlakazeka rolled her eyes and kept quiet. Nona asked her repeatedly who the father was but Hlakazeka remained silent. Then Nona went crazy. She went for the girl, beating her with her open hand and her fists. Hlakazeka did not scream or retaliate. All she did was try to protect her face from the blows. Someone ran to inform the manager who rushed to our hut and found Nona assaulting Hlakazeka. He persuaded Nona to go back to the main house and told Hlakazeka to leave the farm immediately. Nobody knew where she went. She was never heard of again.

By now, I was a fully developed girl with a big bust, a tiny waist and full rounded hips. I was what is aptly referred to as a Zulu ntombi. I had a few suitors whom I ignored because I did not want to invoke Oubaas's wrath. I continued to look after the children and did kitchen chores. The children's playroom was at the far end of the house. It faced north and next to it was a small garden overlooking the mountain with a tiny river at the foot of it.

In winter I often took the children outside and let them enjoy the sunshine and the scent of the flowers in the garden. This became my favourite spot. I loved sitting there and getting lost in my thoughts. I daydreamed about many things. Sometimes I would think of my father and wonder how life would have been for us if there had been no war. I wondered how old he would be now and what he would look like. At times I thought he must be laughing at me, remembering how I had so wanted to meet white people.

I loved this spot for another reason. From here I could see the school in the local village which was attended by African children whose parents were not farm workers. At midday I would see the children playing in the school grounds. I longed to join them and resolved that one day I would do so. I did not know how I would get there but I was determined that the day would come when I would be one of the girls playing in the school yard.

I spent a lot of time in the children's garden. Sometimes when the children were having their nap I sat alone there, musing, or I had my lunch there. One day I was sitting in my favourite place, lost in thought, when suddenly I sensed that there was someone behind me. I turned around slowly. Oubaas was standing behind me. I didn't know how long he had been there. We looked at each other, our eyes locked in a silent stare. I do not know where I got the courage to stare back at him, but I did. For a few seconds we were engaged in this 'eye warfare'.

Eventually he asked, 'What are you doing here? Where are the children?'

'They are inside sleeping,' I answered him. Deep down in my heart I wanted to ask him, 'And what are you doing here watching me?'

'Do you like it here?' he asked.

'Yes,' I answered.

He turned and walked away, leaving me with my mind reeling and asking myself many questions.

I was sure this was not the first time he had watched me surreptitiously. I could tell that he was up to something but I did not know what it was. He had nothing to do with me and my job. My responsibilities were to the children and the kitchen and these chores fell into Nona's ambit. Of course it was his right to stand there and ask me questions about his children but to me it felt out of place.

I soon forgot about the encounter as I continued with my tasks of looking after the children and baking bread until one afternoon when

Oubaas again appeared in the garden. This time he came up to where I was sitting. I don't know what came over me but when I saw him approach I stood up as though I was expecting him. He came close to me and looked me straight in the eye. I stared back at him without blinking. He was breathing loudly through his nostrils. Suddenly he put his hand on my breast and held it. Without thinking, I sank my teeth deep into his ugly hairy arm. He snatched his hand away and raised it to deliver a powerful blow to my face which knocked me off my feet. Everything happened so fast. I felt as though I was having a nightmare, lying on the grass as he kicked me and swore at me, telling me he was going to kill me. 'And if you dare tell Nona that I beat you, I swear I will most certainly kill you,' he said and walked away.

I didn't know what to do. I lay on the grass, writhing in pain. Every part of my body ached. I feared that my ribs were broken. As for my right eye, it stung as though it was about to pop out of its socket. I wondered if I would ever walk again. Then, by some strange miracle, Khosi appeared. She was smiling as she approached me until she saw my face. She asked immediately, 'What happened to you? Who did this to you?'

'Oubaas,' I said, and began sobbing.

'Good grief. Why did he hit you? Did he touch you inappropriately? Oh, my God!'

Slowly I told her what had happened and she listened quietly, occasionally shaking her head in disbelief. 'Ever since Hlakazeka left, he has been touching all of us,' she said. 'I do not know how we are going to stop him from molesting us. I tell you, Oubaas has got out of hand.'

'I don't know about you,' I said, 'but I am not going to allow him to touch me again, ever.'

'How will you do that?' Khosi asked. 'Fight him? He'll simply rape you and then kill you.'

'I will kill him first, I swear on my father's unknown grave. He will never touch me again. I swear I'll kill this animal with my bare hands.'

Khosi helped me to my feet and walked me to our hut. We decided that we were going to tell Nona I had been kicked by a cow. Khosi went to the kitchen and told Nona that I had had an accident. Nona did not waste a minute. I heard her footsteps as I was lying on my grass mat and anticipated even more trouble.

'What happened to you?' she asked. 'And you'd better tell me the truth.'

I didn't answer her. She screamed at me, demanding to know what had happened. Then, suddenly quite calm, she said, 'You people think I am stupid. First Oubaas comes in with a bleeding arm and now you are lying here beaten green and black. What did he want from you? Do you want to end up like Hlakazeka?' She stormed out of the hut.

For days I stayed in the hut convalescing. I realised that for some reason Nona had a soft spot for me, for she gave Khosi some painkillers to give to me and she made sure that I had food brought to me. The other girls were surprised at her reaction. The first two days after the assault were torture. The painkillers did little to relieve my excruciating headache. My eye was so badly injured that I could barely see out of it and my ribs ached with every breath I took. I was in incessant pain. Khosi told me that Oubaas had to go to the doctor to have his arm attended to because the wound had become septic. Khosi asked me what I had used to make Oubaas's arm rot.

'You mean to tell me that your teeth are responsible for the wound on his arm? You must have had something in your mouth. Tell me the truth!' We laughed about it.

I had not seen Oubaas since the assault but Khosi told me that he was going about with his arm in a bandage and that he was in a foul mood most of the time. To my disgust, for days afterwards I kept finding pieces of his flesh embedded between my teeth.

'You know how mean he is,' Khosi said. 'Well, he is even worse. He swears at everyone and threatens to beat us all up, including Nona. We are all worried about what is going to happen to us. Make sure you stay out of his way.'

Of course I had no intention of crossing his path. Nona continued to be most kind to me during those days. She allowed me to remain in our hut. Occasionally the children, especially Kleinbaas, came to see me. They wanted me to come and play with them.

While I was recovering, I had time to think about my fate. And as I became better and regained my strength I also regained my thinking abilities. I knew that I had a formidable enemy in Oubaas and I had to do something. I suspected that he was planning to do something bad to me and I was not prepared to be caught napping. I was mentally ready for anything. I knew we could not both stay alive – either he would kill me or I would kill him. I did not have any physical weapons whereas he had every weapon imaginable to equip himself for hunting expeditions and self-defence.

The more immediate danger for me, as I saw it, was that he had the key to our hut. He could come in at any time of night or day and kill me. I was not afraid to die. On numerous occasions I had stared death in the face. However, I was not prepared to let him kill me like a fly. The one advantage I had over him was that he was not a young man, and I had to make sure that counted in my favour. The few seconds that I had been locked in a scuffle with him I had realised that he was not as strong as he made out. I knew I was strong enough to tackle him, but I also knew that battles were not won by brawn alone. I needed to keep my wits about me. I knew he was smarter than me and I knew he would use devious means to corner me and destroy me. I was the one he was most angry with because I was the only person so far to have inflicted pain on him. Khosi told me that I was the talk of the village. I was a hero to some people and a witch to others who suspected that I used muthi to confront Oubaas in a duel, and that I had inflicted poison when I bit his arm.

I thought long and hard about how I would kill him. Because I was sick I was not in a position to roam about, and in any case I knew he was monitoring my movements. Had I been able to leave my hut, I might have asked one of the young farm workers to lend me a spear. I even thought of collecting sizeable stones and pretending to use them as pillows. I discarded that idea when I recalled how Nona had a habit of checking up on me. I knew I would really have some explaining to do if she discovered stones in our hut.

I had no way of protecting myself and knew that it would be only a matter of time before Oubaas killed me. Finally, I concluded that the only option I had was to flee from the farm.

By now, I knew the area well and could find my way around. What I didn't know was where I would go. The only people I could try to contact were my Makhoba family but I did not know exactly where they lived and I had no idea how to get there. All I remembered was that they were somewhere in Nquthu. I didn't care that Mother had left their homestead unceremoniously; I was one of them and they would have to embrace me. The major drawback to my plan was that leaving the farm meant I would never see my mother and Ndumbutshu ever again. My choice was between staying and being at the mercy of Oubaas, likely to be raped and killed in the near future, or running away to stay alive at the cost of never seeing my mother again.

I chose the latter.

Respite

Like most nights Sis Ahh and I were lying on the bed talking. This was after she had said her prayers. Outside it was raining cats and dogs. The common Zululand storm is often accompanied by awesome thunder and lightning that tends to strike trees, hacking the huge trunks in the middle and leaving them gaping as though a lunatic carrying a big axe was on the rampage. Woe unto anyone walking outdoors at that time; they become easy targets of the raging storm. The locals still strongly believed that witches were capable of attracting lightning and sending it to their enemies, who then caught fire.

As the rain pelted against the window panes and the occasional thunder shook the roof, my mind was racing. Maybe not as fast as the lightning but, as usual, I had many questions nagging my brain. Thank heavens, such storms don't last for ever. They are soon gone, leaving a tranquil silence in their wake.

'Tell me, Sisi,' I said to Ahh, 'did you ever discuss Gogo's life with Mother? Surely she knew that you were aware what had happened to Gogo?'

'Yeah, we did talk about it a lot, especially during the last days of Gogo's life. But you know what? Dad and Mom had decided many years ago not to let you guys know about this.'

'Why?'

'Their rationale was that if any of you knew what the Redcoats and the farmers had done, that information would have sent you straight into the arms of the liberation movements. Remember what was happening in the late 60s and the 70s? With the groundswell of political movements at universities and high

schools, our parents thought the stories about Gogo's suffering at the hands of white people would give you people (to paraphrase Mom, she actually said "you hotheads") more than enough reason to become involved in politics.'

I looked at her and shook my head because what she told me didn't make sense. Our ignorance or lack of knowledge of what had happened to Gogo did not deter us from being politically aware. How could it? There was so much political activity around us, there was no way we could not have been sensitised. There was so much anger in the country – although maybe not to the extent of the events in 1976 when the students declared war on the government and there was so much mayhem and lawlessness. Ours was a different type of groundswell.

We experienced so much blatant injustice. The Nationalist government had entrenched its powers ensuring that Africans had no place in South Africa. They talked of white South Africa and the homelands. Dr Hendrik Verwoerd had just introduced the Bantu Education Act and in retaliation the African National Congress called for a boycott of schools, so for a few days we did not go to school. Sophiatown was being demolished and the ANC held frequent meetings at the communal hall where locals gathered to discuss ways of fighting the laws that were aimed at making Africans foreigners in the land of their forefathers.

After the meetings the people would break into song and the powerful voice of the local activist Ida Mtwana could be heard for miles around. I can still hear her passionate alto voice singing:

Sikhalela izwe lethu
Elathathwa abelungu
Abayeke umhlaba wethu
We lament the loss of our land that was taken by white people. They must leave our land.

How could our parents think we would not be affected by the events unfolding before us? The Boers were flexing their muscles and Africans were reacting in whatever way they deemed fit. There were heated debates between the communities about issues affecting them.

Sophiatown residents were to be forcibly removed to Meadowlands; protests were held, songs such as 'Ons phola hier' – we will live here – were composed. We didn't think that the Boers would actually go ahead and remove people; we thought the old people had enough influence to stop the removals. Then one morning we saw the huge trucks drive into Sophiatown. We watched in disbelief as people's furniture was piled onto the trucks while white soldiers stood by with rifles pointed at the residents loading their valuables. There was a hush as Father Trevor Huddleston walked about offering words of comfort to the people who were leaving and others who were quietly sobbing.

Black parents could not protect their children against that brutality. And yet my parents thought they could pull wool over our eyes by keeping us uninformed about our history.

Then our brother Mzilikazi, the family's blue-eyed boy, the family intellectual, became involved with the Pan Africanist movement and was detained. Our world fell apart.

The news that Mzilikazi together with a number of teachers, including Bishop Stanley Mogoba, had been detained on Poqo activities hit my father badly. He aged within days. We were still living in Western Native Township when the police made a swoop on the PAC branch in Mamelodi township in Pretoria. Father paced the floor and walked about the churchyard late at night like a ghost, talking, mumbling and gesticulating, while Mother was losing her mind imagining what the Boers were doing to her son. She was also concerned about her daughter-in-law Rose, who was alone with their small children. It was a very traumatic time for my family.

'Yes, I remember,' said Sis Ahh. 'I had to come all the way from Zululand to find out what was going on. My worst fear was that the Boers might detain Father as well. Those were the days when the powers that be were known to harass and detain any member of the family as they deemed fit. Fortunately it didn't come to that. But do you know that Sis B worked for the African National Congress as a typist, and her boss was Walter Sisulu?'

'No, you lie! When was that?'

'In the early 1950s. You know she had earlier enrolled as a nurse at the Pretoria General Hospital. While there, she developed a heart defect and could not continue nursing. She came back home to Johannesburg, took a secretarial course and was hired by Sisulu as his personal assistant. But do you know what our parents told the church? They said she was working at the Bantu Men's Social Centre.'

'You mean our parents lied to the church? Why?'

'The Salvation Army church forbade their officers to be involved in politics. They had to lie to protect themselves from the church.'

Now that was news to me. I had been very close to Sis B but I never knew about that part of her life. I was ten years younger than her. By the time I opened my eyes she was working for Dale Outfitters in Plein Street, not far from the Johannesburg railway station. Later on she got a job with some dubious Jewish firm that was involved in an 'insurance' scheme for Africans.

The revelation of this information made me recall an incident in 1960 that had left me baffled. By then our parents had already retired from active service and were living in Zululand. I was living with Mzilikazi and his wife in Pretoria, Sis B was staying in Mofolo with our oldest brother Stanford. Not long after the Sharpeville massacre, I visited Mofolo only to find my siblings were engaged in a cold war. When I enquired what the reason was for the hostilities, Sis B told *me that the Pan Africanist Congress had dropped pamphlets in people's homes instructing them to burn their passes. When Bro Stan found the document under the door, he accused Sis B and her 'cohorts' of distributing the pamphlets. When I questioned Sis B about it she swore she had nothing to do with it. I believed her because I knew her to be apolitical. But of course Bro Stan knew that she had once worked for the ANC and therefore to him she was furthering the aims of the party. Sis B not only denied any knowledge about the distribution of the pamphlets but was disgusted with her brother for linking her with the PAC programme and being vocal about it.*

She said: 'He's telling everybody about this and he has no proof whatsoever. What if the police should learn about this? They will most certainly lock me up and throw the key away.' She began crying.

Fortunately the feud between brother and sister did not last long. They somehow found their way back to each other and the matter was buried. However, in retrospect I find it strange that Bro Stan could not make out the difference between the ANC and the PAC. To him they were one and the same thing. Which reminded me of my crazy aunt who used to describe the two political movements thus: 'whether it is Chardonnay or a Stein, both are white wine'.

So that was what it was all about, skeletons in the cupboard. I knew many households whose rattling skeletons had put families asunder. I had heard many stories about siblings who could not see eye to eye because of political differences. I had heard of couples getting divorced because one spouse did not want to be involved in the political activities of the partner. I had also heard stories of family members selling out on each other.

But that was then, when we were fighting apartheid. We were in a democracy now and people were proud of the role they had played, however small, in eradicating the evil system of apartheid. Stories about who did what abounded.

Narratives that nobody would have dared mention in those years were now keeping the nation spellbound. Some were sad tales of torture in prison and others were downright funny, like the story of one of my township neighbours. He was a colourful character who seemed to know everyone and everything. He claimed he had been arrested for shoplifting and was thrown in a cell at the No. 4 prison which he had to share with PAC activists.

'I was most uncomfortable with these fellows so when the warder came in the morning, I told him: "Baas, ek is 'n dief. Ek weet nie wat soek ek met die mense. Gee my net 'n wapen en wys my waar die geld is, ek sal dit haal. Ek behoort nie met die mense nie." Boss, I'm a thief. I don't know why I'm here with these people. Just give me a weapon and show me where the money is, I'll go and fetch it. I don't belong with these people.' He was released promptly.

If people could tell tales about their involvement in the struggle, or lack thereof, without batting an eyelid, why did my family find the need to be secretive? Sis B and Mzilikazi should have told their stories so that we siblings could also boast of our family members who were 'relevant' in the struggle. Although to be fair to Mzilikazi he sometimes, particularly if he was upset, mentioned aspects of his incarceration. However, this was not something he boasted about.

PART SIX

Escape to Freedom

Once more I was on the road. For the first time in my life I was by myself, with no clear idea as to where I was going. What I knew was that I had to get as far away from the farm as I could and I had to do this as soon as possible.

I left at midnight. It was a clear winter's night, cold with a full moon. I knew at that time of the night everybody would be asleep. I did not even tell Khosi, the only person I was close to on the farm, that I was running away. I had no doubt if I had told her she would have discouraged me. I was determined to leave. I left with only the clothes on my back and one extra jersey.

I did take my knobkerrie though, a fighting stick. It had been specially carved for me by one of the farm boys who thought I needed one to protect myself against snakes when I took the children out for walks in the veld. I took the stick with me to protect myself against the wild animals of the night, or other possible assailants.

Avoiding the main house, I carefully made my way out through the back part of the building. I heard the dogs wake up as I walked past the stables. As soon as they picked up my scent they went back to sleep. I walked on and on, treading carefully past the water tanks, making sure I didn't make a noise. Once I reached the pig sty, I knew I was almost out of danger of being detected by anyone on the farm. Even at that time of the night, the stench from the pigs' dwelling was unbearable.

I was now a few miles away from the main road. I knew that once I reached the road, chances of being spotted were minimal. It was so dark that I could not see my arms let alone my feet, but I managed to pick my way along. Soon I was off Oubaas's property and on the road to Dundee. Even though there was a full moon, the trees lining the road threw nasty images in front of me. This was the time when nocturnal beasts such as jackals, owls and snakes came out prowling for food. I could feel their eyes on me but I suppressed my fear and I walked on. Propelled by the promise of freedom, I trudged along the edge of the road, stumbling on the stones probably unearthed by the horses and wagons that used the thoroughfare. I dared not walk in the middle of the road for fear of being spotted by witches who might abduct and kill me, or cut my tongue and turn me into a zombie.

Although I had not fully recovered from the injuries inflicted during the assault by Oubaas, I was strong enough to withstand the hazards of my escape. I walked on and on, not looking back. By then I had decided to go to the African village school in Dundee. I was going to be part of the group of free children who attended this school.

I crossed the tiny river which separated the farm from the village and soon I was walking on the stretch of road that led directly into the town and which during the day was normally a hive of activity with endless human traffic. It was the main link between the villages around Dundee and the many farms in the area as well as those in the mountains, even as far as Nquthu. Except for the rustle of rats and rabbits in the grass along the road, and the irritating sound of the crickets, the moonlit night was still.

The first ray of sunlight pierced the sky as I took the bend next to the mountain on the road to the town which now came into view. I looked back then trying to gauge the distance I had travelled but I couldn't see anything, not even the silhouette of the farmhouse in spite of the fact that it was a gigantic white-painted structure. Behind me lay darkness, ahead there was light. The town lights were beckoning me and my heart leapt with joy as I felt freedom in my veins. Although I was apprehensive about where I was going because I knew nobody in Dundee, I decided that I would worry about that when I got there.

For the first time since leaving the farm, I wondered about my mother. How would she take the news that I had run away? I felt sorry for her. She had suffered so many difficult and hurtful experiences in her lifetime and by leaving the farm I was adding more pain and grief to her woes. Although I had consciously made the choice to face the possibility of never seeing her and my sister ever again, I was suddenly consumed with doubts and fear. These feelings leapt into my mind and the euphoria of freedom evaporated to be replaced by a terrible feeling of guilt. I was gripped by the fear of failure. How would I cope without my mother, I wondered. Although I had not been living with her, because she stayed outside the main house, she was, however, within reach. I began to question the wisdom of my action, that maybe I should not have run away. For the first time since deciding to flee, I was hit by the magnitude and the ramifications of my decision. I was tempted to turn back, but a voice within me said, 'If you go back now, Oubaas will kill you. Do you want to die?'

I pushed the negative thoughts out of my mind and continued on my journey. I knew that Oubaas would seek his revenge on my mother and the old man. But because there was nothing I could do about that,

I moved on. I was hoping against hope that Oubaas would leave them alone, as they had nothing to do with my leaving. If Oubaas wanted to be honest and fair to the old man and my mother, he would know that they had no influence over me, particularly as I had been living by his rules. I was discouraged from keeping in contact with them and seldom saw them. They could not have influenced me to leave the farm. Although I now knew that Mother hated living on the farm, she had resigned herself to that life.

As I walked on, my mind immersed in thought, my reverie was cut short by the sound of horses pulling a cart. I quickly left the road and hid amongst the bushes. From where I was hiding, I could see two men sitting in the cart as it came closer. Behind the two men, numerous sacks and bags were loaded on the cart. I figured the men were going to the market and I decided to come out of hiding and ask them to give me a lift to town. With both my arms raised, I emerged from the bushes and stood in the middle of the road. When the men saw me they stopped, curiosity registered on their faces. I don't think they expected to see anyone, let alone a girl, coming out of the bushes at that hour. They must have feared that I was a ghost or a witch.

'Hhey, madoda, what is this?' one of the men said to the other. After recovering from the shock of seeing me, they greeted me and looked me up and down, as if to ascertain whether I really was a human being.

The second man asked: 'Are you not the girl from Oubaas?'

'Yes, I am from Oubaas's farm. I am running away. I am going to the school in Dundee.'

They took a good look at me and shook their heads.

The older one said, 'You are badly bruised. Did Oubaas beat you? Is that why you are running away?'

I nodded.

Again the men shook their heads as if in denial of something. The older one said: 'My child, nobody has ever run away from Oubaas. He will hunt you down and when he finds you he will kill you. You think what he did to you was a severe beating. Wait until he finds you, you will wish to die'.

He turned and addressed his companion. 'What do you think we should do? Don't you think we should hide this child between the bags of crops? If Oubaas finds her on the road, he will kill her.'

'No, we can't do that,' said the younger man. 'If he discovers that we helped her to escape he will come to our farm and beat us to a pulp, I tell you. You know that man is crazy. I will have nothing to do with this child. She knew what she was doing when she left the farm. Let's go.'

He began to whistle to the horses and tugged the reins. The older man pulled the reins away from him. An argument ensued between the two men concerning my freedom. The older man was adamant that he was not going to leave me on the road to be found by Oubaas.

'What is wrong with you?' he said. 'This is a child and look what that monster has done to her already. I don't care whether or not he discovers that we assisted her. What matters now is that we must help her. She has suffered too much not to succeed. Besides, I will not have the death of this girl on my conscience.'

Grudgingly, the younger man relented. They alighted from the cart and prepared space for me to hide. I had to lie flat on the back of the cart while they piled bags full of cabbages and beans on top of me. When they were confident I could not be detected, they drove off.

Lying beneath the cabbages was not too uncomfortable – but what was almost unbearable was the smell of the cabbages. Three hours' travel with cabbages on top of me was enough to put me off eating that vegetable for the rest of my life.

We travelled in silence. Occasionally the older man would enquire after my comfort: 'Ntombazana, are you still all right there?'

'Yes, I am,' I answered.

The sun was now up and I knew we were only a few miles from Dundee. I could tell that the road was picking up traffic, as time and again I heard the men greeting people along the way.

Then it happened. At first I thought I was dreaming that I was hearing the sound made by uGagasi's hoofs, Oubaas's horse. The animal came nearer. I froze, my mind in turmoil. Was my life over? I wondered. What were the men going to do or say to Oubaas? Would they betray me? I was more anxious about the reactions of the younger one; I feared that he would not risk his life for me.

Soon the horse and its rider caught up with us. I was relieved that Oubaas was not travelling with the dogs because they would have caught my scent. When Oubaas was parallel with our cart he asked, without greeting the men: 'Anikaboni' ntombazana lapha emgwaqweni?' Have you seen a girl on the road?

The older man answered, 'Cha, Basi. No, Baas.'

'As you would tell me if you had!' said Oubaas. 'I warn you, it will be death for you if you are lying to me.'

The men ignored him as he cantered alongside their cart. I lay as quietly as if I was a corpse. Inwardly, I implored the spirits of all the Makhobas and the Jokos to protect me. Oubaas must have been wondering about the cargo on the cart because the next thing I heard him ask was: 'Where are you going?'

'We are taking fresh produce to the market in Dundee, Mnumzane,' answered the older man.

I almost died. I feared his next move would be to demand to inspect the cart to check whether they were indeed carrying only vegetables to the market. I held my breath and waited for the worst to happen. I knew he would kill me if he found me, but I was prepared to inflict hurt on him before I died. I still had my stick with me. He was not a young man and I had felt the measure of his strength the day we had fought. I knew I could tackle him, unless of course he meant to shoot me. By some grace, he didn't pursue the matter. He travelled along next to us for quite a distance without uttering a word before giving up and galloping away.

We continued quietly on our journey. It was obvious that the two men were shaken by Oubaas's sudden appearance and his questioning of them. Before we reached the town, we came to a village. The men stopped the cart and asked me if I knew where I was going. I told them I didn't, but that I wanted to go to school.

'Are you meeting anyone there?' they asked.

'No. I don't know anybody in this part of the world. I just want to go to school.'

'Look, my girl,' said the older man, 'we are going to make life very simple for you. There is a mission school not far from here. We will take you there. We are doing this because Oubaas may just come back and this time he will definitely want to search the cart.'

I could not disagree. They took me to the school and left me at the gate. I thanked them profusely and walked into the school yard. I looked around. There were many buildings in the yard but there was not a soul in sight. I sat down on the classroom veranda and started to cry. I didn't know what to do with myself. I was alone, I was cold and scared. What would happen to me? Where would I sleep? I was hungry and my body ached. I sobbed myself to sleep.

I was awoken by what seemed to be a shadow over me. When I looked up, I stared into the eyes of a kind-looking man. He was dressed like a white person. Apart from the colour of his skin, which was like mine, he looked like the few white people I had seen visiting the farm. I had never come across an African like him.

All the male farm workers wore worn-out clothing such as old jackets and khaki shirts and trousers. This man was dressed differently. He looked impeccable in a white shirt and a black suit. Beneath the jacket he wore a black waistcoat with tiny pockets. Dangling from one of the pockets was a watch that was similar to the one owned by Oubaas. He stood there looking at me, his thumbs buried in the pockets of his waistcoat while the rest of his fingers danced on his chest. Perched on his nose was a pair of black-framed spectacles. With a benign smile on his clean-shaven face, the man greeted me in isiZulu and asked me what I was doing at the school during the holidays. I looked at him but did not know what to say to him.

He then asked me: 'Where are you from?'

'I have run away from Oubaas's farm. I want to attend school.'

'Where are your parents? Do they know you have run away?' The kind man looked perplexed as he rattled off questions, one after the other.

'I don't have parents. My father died in the war. He was killed by the

Redcoats. His name was Makhoba and he was King Cetshwayo's most trusted induna belonging to the iNgobamakhosi regiment. My mother is now married to one of Oubaas's workers. I have not seen her in months. I was allowed to visit her only infrequently. She does not know that I have run away.'

'Lord have mercy!' said the man shaking his head. 'Get up. Let's go to the house. Have you eaten anything today?'

'No.'

The man watched me rise from the floor. He noticed that I had difficulty getting to my feet. I was stiff from lying buried under the cabbages, my ribs had not completely healed and my whole body was sore. Again he shook his head, then he took my hand and helped me to my feet. He led me to his house, which was close to a church next to a graveyard. He opened the kitchen door and allowed me to enter while calling to his wife.

'Nkosikazi, nkosikazi, where are you?'

His wife appeared straight away and asked, 'What's the matter? Why do you sound so agitated?'

'Oh! My dear, come and meet this child. Listen to what she has to say.'

His matronly wife was well dressed in a long full skirt covered with an apron. She came up to me and took a good look at me. I was quite a sight after the hours I had spent lying under bags of vegetables. I stood there looking dishevelled, my hair matted and peppered with strands of sacking. As if that was not enough, I had also picked up dust on my skirt while lying on the classroom veranda. The bruises on my face were still visible.

The first thing she said was, 'My child, who did this to you?'

I looked down at the floor and replied, 'Oubaas.'

'Who is Oubaas?'

'He is the farmer I have run away from. He beat me and kicked me all over,' I said lifting up my dress and revealing the bruises around my ribcage. I was not even conscious of the fact that I was not wearing underwear. At the farm, knickers were not part of our supply.

'Stop, my child, that's enough,' said the man.

His wife came closer to me and put her arms around me. I broke down and cried. She also began to cry. Her husband came up to us and held us both, comforting me and asking us to stop crying. He then asked me to tell them who I was and everything about myself.

I began to tell my story. Once I had started, I couldn't stop. I told them everything, from the moment we went to hide in the mountains right up to my escape from the farm.

When I had finished talking, the man said, 'Nkosikazi, let us pray. We need to pray to get the strength and guidance of God to help this child.'

His wife went down on her knees and clasped her hands together in front of her bosom. The man knelt on one knee next to a chair and began praying. I didn't know what to do. I didn't know what prayer was. I had never heard of prayer because I had never been to church. Nobody at the farm went to church. I just stood there, looking at the two people, the man speaking to some person he kept calling Father. He spoke with his eyes closed while his wife, also with eyes closed, softly nodded along. When he had finished talking to whoever he was addressing, he said to his wife, 'Nkosikazi, this child hasn't eaten anything today. Please find her something to eat.'

The woman quickly prepared me a lunch of sour milk and uphuthu, a popular Zulu dish of crumpled pap made out of maize. While I was eating, the couple adjourned to an inner room.

When they returned, the man said: 'You said you wanted to attend school here, what standard have you passed?'

'What is that?' I asked.

'Have you attended school at all?' he asked, obviously surprised at my answer.

'No,' I replied.

'How old are you?' he asked. When he realised I could not understand his question, he rephrased it: 'When were you born?'

'Mother told me that I was born when Somtseu gave King Cetshwayo the ultimatum to disband his regiments,' was my reply.

The man shook his head and said it would be difficult to guess my birth date because Somtseu had given Cetshwayo ultimatums on numerous occasions.

'Nkosikazi, this is going to be a difficult one,' he said. 'How old do you think this child is? If she is able to remember events about the war so clearly, she must have been about eight or ten years old. The war was in January 1879. We are now in 1890. Could she be nineteen or twenty-one years old?'

Turning to me he said, 'We would like you to stay with us. I will inform the church about you and we will see what to do about school.'

★

And so I stayed with the couple and I got to know that the husband was a Lutheran Church priest. They had two teenage daughters who were

185

away at boarding school. His wife bought me clothes which included knickers. They gave me a room and a bed to sleep in. I refused to sleep on the bed fearing that I would fall off. For many weeks I slept on the floor until their daughters came back from school and persuaded me to use the bed. I helped with the cleaning and the cooking in the kitchen. Gradually I forgot about the miserable life I'd led at the farm. The family was kind to me and I was happy.

The first Sunday after my arrival, the couple took me to church where I was asked to address the congregation about my situation. By the time I'd finished speaking, all the women in the church were in tears. Some were sobbing openly as if they were at a funeral. The male congregants were stony-faced and solemn. On realising how trauma-tised the congregation was, a member of the church choir started to sing a hymn. Gradually, one by one, the congregation joined in the singing which eased the sadness away. I received a lot of support and love from the members of this church. They told me they were in awe of my cour-age and the way in which I had overcome so many difficulties in my young life.

The Reverend and his wife introduced me to Christianity. They told me Bible stories and showed me pictures of Jesus and his disciples. I had many questions to ask about Christianity which they answered willingly. They, in turn, never seemed to tire of asking me about life at the farm. They were intrigued by what I had experienced both at the farm and in the wilderness hiding from the Redcoats. I was open to them about my life and that endeared me to them. For the first time in years I felt safe and loved. I attended Bible classes every night until they decided that I was ready to be baptised. One Sunday I was taken to church to be christened and was given the name Margaretta. The transformation from being a traditional Zulu woman to being a Christian was now complete.

The congregation was jubilant at my conversion, but I was miserable. I felt I had betrayed my family and the entire Makhoba clan. The price I paid for becoming a Christian was too high because it meant I had to forgo everything I had believed in and I feared that it would impact negatively on my life. I looked back to the days I had spent on the farm and concluded that even though it was the worst time of my life, I had not been made to change. I had not been subjected to any attempt at spiritual transformation. Nona and Oubaas had not interfered with my beliefs – they did not care if their workers worshipped their ancestors or not, as long as they did their work.

Living with these Christians would have been pure bliss except for their condemnation of my ancestral beliefs which they described as demonic. This made me unhappy and confused and I felt I was no different from the deserters who had abdicated from Zulu life and joined white people. I began to question whether running away from the farm had been the right thing to do. The Reverend and his wife had embraced me and given me love and provided for me in ways I never thought anyone could, but by imposing their Christian beliefs on me, they had taken away a chunk of my soul.

A short while after I had been baptised, the Reverend was approached by one of the congregants, a widow named MaNkosi. She had grown-up daughters who were married and lived far from her and she said she would like me to stay with her because she lived alone. When the Reverend informed me of MaNkosi's request, I consented. I knew her to be a loving old lady and a devout Christian and so I moved into her homestead.

She soon noticed that I didn't know enough about Christian life and made it her business to educate me. She taught me hymns and the various psalms in the Bible which I had to memorise. Every evening, before going to sleep, we would say the Lord's Prayer together.

MaNkosi lived in a village that was similar to our homesteads in Shiyane, except that her huts were not built of grass. They were mud structures with grass thatched roofs and they even had windows. Although she was advanced in years, she was still a very industrious woman. She worked in her fields where she had planted maize, sorghum, beans and amadumbe. She had cows that were looked after by a young fellow whom she paid for his services.

It was easy for me to adapt to her lifestyle. I accompanied her everywhere she went; I helped her in the fields; I worked in the house and I cooked. She was astonished by the type of food I was able to prepare.

One day I took some milk to the little hut we used as a pantry. I skimmed the cream off and deposited it in a separate container. I was going to make butter. I made the preparations for a couple of days without telling her. When the butter was ready, I presented it to her. She was so surprised and happy; she clapped her hands and exclaimed: 'Ye-hhe-ni! Where did you learn to make butter? You are amazing,' she said hugging me. I told her I had been taught by Nona at the farm.

One day the boy who looked after the cattle did not turn up for work. It was reported that he was sick. I realised that the calves would suckle their mothers' udders dry, and there would be no milk for the day so I decided to do something to remedy the situation. I took the milk can and the milking ropes and went to the kraal where I separated the calves from the heifers, fastened the heifers one by one and began milking them. MaNkosi was amazed when I returned to the hut with the can brimming with milk. Smiling as she thanked me, she asked: 'Did you learn how to milk cows on the farm?'

'No,' I replied. 'My father taught me how to milk a cow. He had no sons so he taught me all the things that boys do in a home.'

MaNkosi was beside herself with joy. I had brought in more milk than the hired boy had been able to. With the surplus I made butter, this time in a larger container. I also made cheese. MaNkosi took some to the priest's home and neither he nor his wife could contain their surprise and joy. The Reverend's wife asked MaNkosi if I could teach the church women how to make butter. The church women met for prayers on Thursday afternoons and I joined them afterwards and conducted my classes. I taught them everything I knew about cooking, including baking cakes. For baking, we dug a deep hole in the ground and built a fire in it, above which we placed a clay pot. This improvised oven would be above the logs of fire and also provide a stove. I also taught them how to make soap.

Soon I became the darling of the village – everyone talked about 'the clever runaway farm girl'. Some women were so happy with my teaching them what they referred to as 'sophisticated cooking' that they brought me presents of live chickens, clay pots and grass mats. MaNkosi beamed from ear to ear.

One day MaNkosi told me that her cousin would be visiting and asked me to help her prepare a special meal for him. She was very excited at the prospect of his visit and I realised that he must be a very important person to her. She even slaughtered a goat for the occasion.

I immediately got down to the business of cooking, starting with kneading dough to make idombolo steam bread, and cooking the porridge for brewing mahewu, the sour maize porridge drink. As MaNkosi did not have a stove, all the cooking was done on the hearth in the floor. The next item we had to prepare was the roast leg of goat. Nona had taught me how to do this over an open fire. I patiently sat next to the hearth, stoking the fire and turning the leg of goat until it was golden brown. By the time the meat was cooked, my eyes were red from inhaling smoke from the fire and I smelled like ash. Later MaNkosi boiled the amadumbe, while I baked the bread.

Her cousin arrived in the late afternoon. He was from somewhere in Durban. He was a very impressive-looking man who carried himself with dignity. I thought he was royalty. He had fine facial features, and a full moustache; he was elegant and soft-spoken. Like the Reverend, he wore smart European clothes. MaNkosi told me he was a devout Christian and would be delivering a sermon in the church the next day. I was told that his village had not been affected by the war, yet he knew what had happened to the people across the Tugela River and not only sympathised with them but assisted in whatever way he could. He was well travelled, had been to many countries and had met great leaders of the world. MaNkosi introduced him to me as John Langalibalele Dube.

We sat down to eat. John Dube enjoyed the meal and congratulated MaNkosi, stating that he had on previous occasions enjoyed eating at her house but this time she had outdone herself. MaNkosi told him that she had very little to do with the meal. With a complimentary wave of her hand in my direction, she told him that the entire preparation of the meal had been my responsibility. Looking surprised, Dube turned to me and asked, 'Where did you learn to cook so well?'

'I was taught by the missus at the farm where I used to live.'

'You will have to write down the recipes for me. I would like to try some of the dishes myself.'

'I'm sorry, I'm afraid that I cannot write,' I answered.

'What do you mean, you can't write? Haven't you been to school?'

'No, I haven't.'

'Dade, Sister,' the man addressed MaNkosi, 'how come this child hasn't been to school? How can you live with a child and deny her an education when there is a school on your doorstep?'

'Wait. Before you get all worked up, let me tell you the story of this child.'

MaNkosi began telling my story, starting with how I had escaped from the farm, ended up at the mission and how she had asked the missionaries to let me be her companion because she lived alone.

Dube listened in utter silence while MaNkosi spoke. When she had finished he said: 'Dade, this is a very sad story. Unfortunately there are many people, young and old, who have suffered with the arrival of the white people. That is why it is so important that we Africans should unite to find a way of fighting this scourge of domination and poverty and the best way to do this is through education. I beg you to take this child to school. Without an education she will for ever be at the mercy of other people.'

The following day was Sunday and we all went to church to listen to the sermon Dube delivered. The service was well attended because he was a renowned preacher. That Sunday morning I found Dube so inspiring that for once I listened carefully to the sermon. It was based on the persecution of the Christians by Saul. He drew a parallel between the persecution of Africans by whites and furthermore that of Semites by those who, like Saul, could not tolerate any deviation from their own beliefs. For the first time this Christian thing began to make sense to me. I realised that the Zulus were not the only nation that had been discriminated against and been annihilated by conquerors.

After church, Dube held counsel with leading personalities in the community such as teachers, nurses and traditional leaders. He left the next day but not before telling MaNkosi that he hoped that on his next visit he would find that I was attending school.

Getting me enrolled at school proved to be a tricky task. I was over twenty years old, older than the oldest child at the local primary school. The principal told MaNkosi that he could not admit me to the school but he would enrol me for the afternoon classes which were held for the boys who looked after the livestock.

These young men were really too old to be starting primary school. Some of them were also too old to be cattle herders. Their contemporaries had left the villages to work in the cities and those who had stayed behind and were still tending cattle, sheep and goats still clung to the old Zulu traditions. They called themselves Abakhephehleli, self-styled Zulu regiments who longed for the old ways when young men were at the battle front. The regiment system had been officially disbanded and there was nothing in its place. Most people in the villages had become Christians and dressed like white people, but Abakhephehleli continued to wear ibheshu as well as all the adornments that enhance Zulu attire.

The Abakhephehleli travelled in groups to weddings and other rituals. When these young men were on a serious outing, they wore their best ibheshu and beads around their necks and adorned their arms with birds' feathers. They carried dangerous sticks that were also decorated with colourful beads. At weddings, they engaged in dance competitions, which invariably ended up in stick fights. In most cases these festivities culminated in some of the young men being injured; some even died of their injuries. Most of the skirmishes occurred when one of the couple getting married was from another part of the region. Almost all villages had groups of young men who were Abakhephehleli and they were unpopular because they appeared wild and crude at a time when the rest of the nation was licking the wounds incurred during the war. Communities wanted to live in peace.

I was the first and only girl to attend the literacy class with the young men. When I first joined these men tried to make fun of me. Some even went as far as saying I had enrolled in their class in search of a husband. I ignored their silly and sometimes caustic comments and concentrated on the lessons. In no time I had learned to write and read my vowels. I moved on to concentrate on the rest of the alphabet and was soon able to combine a vowel and a consonant – Ma – Me – Mi – Mo – Mu, I read. My classmates watched in wonderment as I started reading *Masihambisane,* the Zulu reader for beginners. From that time onwards I read any book, pamphlet or magazine that I could lay my hands on. I befriended the girls in the neighbourhood who attended the local school and they coached me in reading. Soon I was able to read the Zulu Bible. In the evenings when MaNkosi and I had evening prayers I would read from the Bible and she would interpret the scripture and pray.

John Dube continued to visit us. He followed my literacy progress with interest and he also showed interest in my past, spending a great deal of time asking me questions about my experiences during the war and my sojourn on the farm. At times he took notes as I was talking and whenever I seemed befuddled he would say: 'Take your time. Breathe and think. This is very important history for our people. The generations that come after us will want to know how we became vagrants in our own country.'

Amongst other things that he deemed important, Dube asked me how I felt about leaving my mother and sister behind. I told him it made me sad but there was nothing I could do about it; for me, it was a case of survival. I told him that I feared more for Ndumbutshu, my sister, because I knew that when she was grown up she would be expected to take my place at the farm and Oubaas would be vindictive towards her.

Dube asked me what I thought of the possibility of having my mother and sister abducted. I told him it was impossible to snatch them away from the farm because the property was under the strictest security. He suggested we could organise some of the farm workers to help in the kidnapping but I told him that except for Khosi, there was nobody at the farm I trusted. Oubaas had put the fear of God in the hearts of his labourers. Instead of helping my mother and sister escape, they would most likely inform Oubaas of our intentions. But the biggest snag about the abduction proposal lay with me. I had been gone for so long that I didn't know where it was. Nor did I know what the farm was called. Dube abandoned the idea when he realised I was not too keen on it.

By this time I was well informed about current affairs. I knew that the invaders had abducted King Cetshwayo and taken him to their country where they paraded him in front of their queen before bringing him back to our land. Cetshwayo had since died and so had his successor, his son Dinuzulu. The king who was then on the throne was Solomon, son of Dinuzulu, and he was king in name only. The invaders had stripped him of all powers. This act of emasculating the king had incensed many Zulus, Christians as well as non-believers. There was a great deal of anger and helplessness in the land. The church leaders preached about this and asked the congregations to pray for the return of the Zulu monarchy.

Our biggest source of information and news was a monthly pamphlet published by Dube called *Isitha somuntu nguye uqobo lwakhe* – a person is one's own worst enemy. This pamphlet, popularly called *Isitha* (the enemy), was circulated by the churches.

Dube wrote powerful articles criticising the wrongs committed by Africans, such as blaming all their problems on white people; he chided them for being lazy and for choosing easy options, and he stressed the value of acquiring an education. He also wrote about what was happening to the people working on the farms and about the people who had lost their land and were leading the lives of vagrants. The pamphlet informed us about the frustrations experienced by King Dinuzulu and later by King Solomon. Most importantly, the hard-hitting editorials stressed the urgent need for unity amongst Africans.

On one of his visits Dube came in the company of a friend. This man was as suave as Dube and even better looking. He was dark with a broad flat nose and chubby cheeks which revealed dimples when he spoke or smiled. He was tall and elegant. His jet-black crop of hair was combed backwards with a short furrow starting at the temple. I was instantly smitten. He got off his horse, adjusted his jacket and dusted off his jodhpurs. I'd never seen such a handsome fellow. With his smiling eyes, he was easy-going and told many jokes. He was introduced to me as Stefaan Mavundla, an evangelist from Isikhwebezi in Northern Zululand. He and Dube spent the evening with us and we served them dinner which they enjoyed. The next day we all went to church and Mavundla preached the sermon. I do not remember what it was about. Although I recall that it was moving I could not concentrate on what he was saying, so mesmerised was I by his good looks and pleasant demeanour.

As usual, after church Dube and his friend joined MaNkosi and me for lunch before attending a meeting with leading members of the community. The Anglo-Boer War had ended and there was talk that the white people were forming a government which would exclude Africans. Not even King Dinuzulu was privy to what the white people were planning. By then, King Dinuzulu had been banished to the Transvaal where he died in 1913, and in 1916 his son King Solomon ascended the throne. Dube reported to the community and the chiefs on the political developments in the region. Of great concern to everyone was the future of the king. What role would he play now that the foreigners were hatching a new political dispensation for themselves?

There was a sprinkling of white Christians in and around Pietermaritzburg who were concerned about this development, but they were few and far between. Protestations from people in Pietermaritzburg came to naught. Zulu people had to do something to save their land from being usurped by whites. The meeting went on until late at night.

The next day, Dube and Mavundla mounted their horses and left, with Mavundla promising that he would be coming back soon.

★

Indeed, Mavundla came back sooner than I had anticipated. We had lunch and then he had a private meeting with MaNkosi before leaving. I was baffled and disappointed by his behaviour for he ignored me completely. It was as though I was not there. I had hoped that he would stay longer. After he had gone, I was surprised to notice that MaNkosi seemed to be in a jovial mood and sang as she went about her chores. She was always good natured and given to telling funny stories and making fun of everybody around her, but that afternoon she was more animated than usual.

Later in the evening, after we had had supper and said our prayers, MaNkosi said: 'Ndodakazi, daughter, I have something to tell you. Mavundla has requested me to ask you to marry him.'

You could have knocked me down with a feather. For a moment I didn't know what to think, let alone what to say. I stared at her in amazement. I had fallen in love with the man but my thoughts had not ventured as far as thinking about marriage.

After what seemed like an eternity, I found my voice. It came out raspingly, as though it was not mine. 'U–u–u–thini? What are you saying?' I asked her.

'Yes, Mavundla wants you to be his wife. What do you say to that?'

'I don't know,' I said.

That evening MaNkosi and I spoke until late, discussing the pros and cons of Mavundla's marriage proposal. MaNkosi was so taken up by Mavundla that one could swear that it was her hand that he had asked for. She told me that she had informed Mavundla about my history and that he had received the news with sadness, and had assured her that he would look after me well. Eventually I had to go to bed. But it took a

long time for the excitement of the proposal to subside and it was some
hours before I fell asleep.

The next day, after completing my domestic chores, I told MaNkosi
that I was going to buy beads at the shop.

'What do you need beads for?' she asked me.

'I want to make ucu, a love-string, for Mavundla.' I saw MaNkosi's
face light up.

'Aha! So you will marry him,' she said laughing and ululating at the
same time. She then took me in her arms and kissed me on both cheeks,
saying: 'Wadla Mavundla.' Mavundla you've won. 'I am pleased for you,
my daughter. He is a good man. He will make you happy.'

I bought the beads and made a beautiful love necklace using red,
white and green beads which were the colours from my original village of Shiyane. I wore the beads around my neck until Mavundla came
visiting again.

This time he came in the company of Dube and two other men. After
a meal, they adjourned to another hut where they held a meeting with
MaNkosi. Later on I was called into the hut. As I entered I was immediately aware of the energy that pervaded the room. I was greeted by the
men's smiling faces, their eyes beaming with joy. They looked at me as
though I was a vase filled with beautiful flowers, and while they did so
I kept my eyes glued to the floor. I dared not raise them. Even though I
could not see their faces and therefore could not read their expressions,
I could somehow feel that they approved of me. I felt the love.

MaNkosi was the first to speak.

'My child, I have had a discussion with these men who are here with
Mavundla who is asking for your hand in marriage. He would like you

to be his wife, to draw him water to drink when he is thirsty, to cook
and feed him. What do you say?'

With my eyes still fixed on the floor, I took the beads off my neck,
went over to where Mavundla was seated and placed the necklace around
his neck. I said: 'I am yours, Mavundla, Ngema, Mthiyane, wena wesilo
esimadevu esingasekuya ekhakonina ngoba bayoswela ukuthi basanga
ngaphi. Mngwemkhulu ...' I rattled off his clan name's praises.

Everybody clapped their hands. MaNkosi ululated and Mavundla
stood up and did the Zulu dance saying:

'Kwa'thangi giye mina, ngagiya mina,'
I feel like dancing, I am dancing
'Ngadla mina,'
I have won
'Ngiyabonga Makhoba, Joko.'
Thank you, Makhoba, Joko.

The men's jubilation took me by surprise. I had laboured under the
impression that educated Christian gentlemen frowned on our Zulu
ways. I had not imagined the simple act of presenting my fiancé with
a love necklace would elicit such excitement. For me, making the love
necklace was the only way I knew to express my love for Mavundla. I
had no clue what Christian women did to show acceptance of a marriage proposal but I certainly did not think it would evoke such delight
and pride in these polished gentlemen.

Later that afternoon, Mavundla and I took a stroll down the gravel
road towards the church. Mavundla talked all the time. He was like

a little boy with a new toy. Animatedly, he told me where he came from and what had happened to his family. We walked past the church towards the open space behind the building, a place that served as a venue for functions. This was where wedding celebrations were held; where the Christmas celebrations were held when the local community got together to exchange gifts, small or large, which they hung on the branches of the trees with the names of the recipients written on them; where local singing groups rendered musical items, and where people working in the city back home on holiday got a chance to show off the latest fashions; a place where lovers met and sometimes where hearts were broken as liaisons ended. The venue was also used by the schools to hold music eisteddfods. The spot was full of trees that were home to a myriad of birds that could be heard chirruping and tweeting at any time of the day. Here it was normal to see rabbits, mice or squirrels scampering as they sought a place to hide, or a stray goat munching on the leaves of the shrubs. In some ways the place was a hive of activity and in another way it was a sanctuary for those who sought peace and quiet.

We slowly and carefully made our way towards one of the large trees, avoiding thorny bushes along the way, and making sure there was no cow dung or goat droppings on the grass. For a place which was usually abuzz with bird songs and cricket sounds, the peace that seemed to pervade it that late afternoon was unusual. It seemed to welcome us as though it was conspiring with us towards the new life that was unfolding ahead of us.

We reached a clearing under the huge tree. Mavundla took both my hands and gently motioned to me to sit down. He did not let go of my hands until I was comfortably seated on the lush grass. I was shaking like a leaf. I did not know what to do. I had never been so close to a man, let alone held a man's hand. I think he could see that I was nervous and, being older than me and being a man of the world, he allayed my fears and nervousness by talking continuously.

'You must realise that I am a poor man,' he said. 'You are marrying someone who has no property. All I have is my undying love and a promise that I will work hard to look after you.'

What could I say? I had lost my tongue. I simply listened to what he was saying, admiring his dimples that appeared time and again as he spoke.

We talked until the moon rose and we had to go back home.

★

Mavundla paid a token lobola to MaNkosi and left to prepare for our wedding. MaNkosi and the church women got together to plan my wedding. They took me to a dressmaker who made me a beautiful wedding gown. It was a long, flowing white lace dress with satin loops all around the skirt and a tight-fitting waist.

Although ours was to be a Christian marriage, on the morning of my wedding day MaNkosi woke me before dawn and took me to the river to bathe. As she rubbed soap on me, she spoke incessantly to my ancestors, imploring them to guide me and protect me on my new journey to womanhood. Afterwards we went back to her homestead, but we did not enter the hut. Instead we went to the cattle pen where we were joined by some of the elderly ladies from the church who were part of the group that was helping MaNkosi prepare for the wedding. MaNkosi led us into the kraal. I was surprised that she was adhering to the Zulu tradition of invoking the presence of the ancestors on the morning of my wedding. If I had any doubts about her love, her actions that morning confirmed to me that she was the mother I had lost.

When I later asked her why she had taken me into the Nkosi kraal where there weren't any Makhoba ancestors, her answer was: 'My child, the spirits of our departed are everywhere and in harmony with us. Besides, I took you into my house from the wilderness and raised you as my child. The Nkosi fathers and grandmothers have been looking after you ever since.'

After the detour to the cattle kraal we went into the hut. My head was reeling. The ritual had reminded me once more of who I was. I was a Zulu maiden about to embark on the most important journey of my life. I couldn't help but remember where I came from and I began to miss my people, my parents in particular. I wondered about my father. How proud he would have been at that moment. For some time I had a lump in my throat. I felt like going outside and screaming. I was tempted to spend some time holding my habitual conversations with myself but I realised that I did not have the luxury of doing so as I was expected at the church in two hours' time. I managed to control my emotions and stayed calm by thinking about my fiancé and the wonderful life lying ahead of us.

The women served me a sumptuous breakfast which I did not enjoy because I was over-anxious about the day. One of the elderly ladies sat next to me making sure that I at least ate something. The other women lectured me about how I must conduct my life as a married woman, stressing repeatedly that I would now belong to Mavundla and how I must love and respect him and never question his actions or decisions.

After we had finished eating, my maid of honour asked the women to allow me to get ready for church. She escorted me to another hut where she helped me into my wedding gown. By ten o'clock, I was ready to go to the church. I was to be there at eleven o'clock. The church bells started ringing. Unlike the usual sombre sound heard on Sunday mornings, this time the bells pealed cheerfully. I smiled. The time had come for me to join my husband.

My bridesmaids and I were taken to a wagon drawn by four horses and driven by a man who was colourfully dressed with a kaleidoscope of plumage on the wide brim of his sombrero-like hat. I later learned that he was a rickshaw man from Durban hired by Mavundla specifically to take me to the church in style. When we arrived at the church we were greeted by school children who were on their break. The little girls clapped their hands in glee when they saw me dismount from the carriage and commented loudly about how beautiful I looked. I admit that I felt like a princess as I walked towards the church, my wedding gown swaying around me as though I was a peacock. I had eight bridesmaids, all members of the church choir. Although their dresses were not ankle length like mine, they looked resplendent in their puffed sleeved dresses.

As we entered the church yard, we could hear the choir singing. They sounded like angels as they sang the famous Christian song: 'Vuka, Vuka we Deborah, vuk'u hlabelel'ngoma' (Wake up, Deborah and sing a song). Everybody stood up when I and my bridal entourage walked into the church to 'oohs and aahs' from the congregation. With my eyes fixed on the floor, I slowly walked to the front of the church where Mavundla was standing regally next to his best men who were dressed in black suits and white shirts. He looked dashing in his black breeches and jacket with broad belts across his chest and waist and well-polished knee-high boots.

Our wedding took place on a Wednesday before noon and was attended by all kinds of people ranging from the locals and fellow worshippers to educated men in suits, accompanied by their wives in all their finery. Unfortunately for us, Dube was away on some fund-raising business overseas. However, he remembered us and brought us a present from his trip when he returned.

Mavundla had not spared anything in making his wedding a day to be remembered. He had even imported a priest from Pietermaritzburg, a friend of his, to conduct the marriage service. He turned out to be an interesting fellow who had the congregation in stitches, making jokes about what married couples often do or don't do. After we had taken our vows, Mavundla surprised everyone by suddenly breaking into song. In his conquering, booming tenor, he sang a well-known song:

Uma uthokoza, bonga, bonga,
njengenyoni enhle, hlabelela.
Ukuhlabelela kuyamthokozisa, odabukileyo, hlabelela.
When you are happy give thanks, like a pretty bird sing,
singing makes even a sad person happy.

The congregation clapped their hands in glee after the song but the one who had the last laugh was the priest who said: 'Mavundla, you are not the only one who can sing. May the bride sing for us.'

I took a deep breath and began singing the chorus from a hymn,

'Count your blessings, name them one by one'. Before I had finished, the entire congregation had joined me in the singing and everyone was in the mood for the wedding party.

The wedding party was held at MaNkosi's homestead where there was food and beer galore. Afterwards I got down to packing. My possessions now included the presents the women from the church had given me. Parting with MaNkosi was the hardest thing I had to do. I was leaving the woman who had taken me into her house and treated me like her own daughter. I promised her that I would visit her often and Mavundla swore to her that he would look after me. We both cried as we kissed and said our goodbyes.

PART SEVEN

The Road Ahead

When the sun rose, I was on the road once more. But this time I was not alone, and I wasn't running away from anyone or anything. I was with my husband Mavundla, and we were on our way to start a new life as missionaries at KwaCeza Lutheran Mission. Everything seemed to be going my way. I was a new bride, married to one of the most eligible bachelors in the region. He was good looking, a Christian, educated, and a Zemtiti.

The Zemtitis – 'exempted' – was an elite class of Zulu men who, because of their education and wealth, were exempted from carrying the normal pass book which other African men had to have on their person at all times. The Zemtitis were not expected to produce the pass book on demand by a policeman. It is an understatement to say exempted Africans were proud of their status. The only snag was that they did not have a mark on their bodies to indicate their status. Needless to say, overzealous policemen often did not bother to check if the African they were stopping was exempted or not. As far as the police were concerned, all African males were to produce the pass book at their demand. For a Zemtiti, there was no worse humiliation than to be stopped by the police in this fashion.

I had come a long way from living in the caves in the mountains to being wooed by and married to a good man. I had also come a long way from walking about semi-clad in a hide skirt and ibhayi to wearing foreigners' clothes. I had at last come a devastatingly long way from believing and worshipping ancestors to being a Christian. Through the eye-opening sermons of Langalibalele, his insistence that I be educated, my husband's sermons and his missionary work and the endless kindness shown to me by true Christians, I had become a devout Christian and held on to that faith with every fibre and breath of my body.

Occasionally I would think of the road I had travelled and realised how lucky and blessed I was. I sometimes thought of the many people who had died of hunger in the mountains, of the many who were killed by the Redcoats. I thought of those I had left behind at the farm; people who would never live a free life, who would never stay on their own property and cultivate their own land; people who would always be owned by somebody.

Hardly a day went by that I did not think about Oubaas and his mean-spiritedness. I thought about him and his cruel ways, like the punishment he meted out to any worker who transgressed any of his rules. There were also hair-raising accounts of what he did to anyone who overslept. These stories were told to me by the girls I shared the hut with at the farm. Fortunately I never experienced his wrath for oversleeping because I could control my sleeping moments. This was partly the result of being on the run for so long and having to stay awake. During our flight from cave to cave through the wilder parts of Zululand until we were taken in by the Ngebeza community, oversleeping was not a luxury one could entertain.

Everyone who lived on the farms around the Dundee area knew of Oubaas's cruelty towards the people living and working on his farm. Despite the criticism it invoked from some of the landlords there were, however, farmers who did enlist his help when there was a 'kaffir' to be disciplined. The most popular ruse the farmers used when disciplining a worker was to beat the worker and then write a note to Oubaas, instructing him to 'give bearer a hiding because he is a cheeky kaffir'. This note was given to the worker, who was obviously illiterate, and the farmer instructed him to deliver it in person and 'wait for the answer'. On receiving and reading the letter, Oubaas would then beat the worker to a pulp.

Yet at other times when I thought about Oubaas, I found I couldn't help but suppress a chuckle, thinking of what I had done. I was the only person who had managed to escape from the farm and had lived to tell the story. How I wished I were a fly and could visit the farm and hear what Oubaas and everybody else had to say about me; about biting his arm and then escaping. Whenever I was consumed by such thoughts I would remember what my father had said, namely, that I would triumph over any adversity. Hadn't he told me that I was born of brave stock and that I should not shy away from any challenge? I was indeed my father's daughter.

Other people who were ever present in my mind were my mother and my little sister Ndumbutshu, and I often wondered what had happened to them.

I assumed that Mother, if she was still alive, was most probably agonising about what could have happened to me and, knowing the type of man Oubaas was, I had no doubt that because of my running away from the farm, he had given her a rough time. I often mused about what Mother would think of my husband. Would she approve of him? Would she be happy and as proud of him as I was? I imagined Mother would be old by then and I wondered if she was at all wrinkled.

I meditated about what my sister looked like now. When we were still living as a family many people said that even though I had my father's build and fair complexion, I looked like my mother and my sister looked like my father. Eventually I refused to dwell on these depressing thoughts as there was nothing I could do about the situation. I chose rather to think about the new life I had embarked on.

Moving to KwaCeza seemed a brave and natural step in my life, although I had no idea what I was in for. Nor did I know much about the man I had married. It did not take me long to realise that while Mavundla had a strong Christian faith, he was first and foremost a politician and a man of the cloth second. I should have taken my cue from his alliance with Langalibalele.

Mavundla didn't say much about his past except to mention he was an orphan, and that his father had died during the 1856 'battle of the children', an event which led to his family, like many others in the Usuthu region, being displaced.

Zulu people referred to this war as 'impi yabantwana' (the battle of the children) because it was a confrontation between the king's children. Two of King Mpande's sons – Prince Cetshwayo and Prince Mbuyazi – wanted to succeed their father as king of the Zulus.

The conflict between the sons was of King Mpande's making. Initially he had chosen Prince Cetshwayo to be his successor. It is not known why he suddenly reneged on this decision and wanted his other son, Prince Mbuyazi, to succeed him. There were claims that Mbuyazi's mother, who was one of King Mpande's wives, had influenced him to change his mind. King Mpande then pitted his sons against each other in the hope that Mbuyazi would kill Cetshwayo. King Mpande also anticipated that should the worst scenario occur, such as the two men killing each other, then another son, Mthonga, could succeed him. King Mpande's resolve not to have Cetshwayo as king of the Zulus was so strong that he is often quoted as saying, 'In Zululand, what one cannot acquire with an open hand, one has to get by using one's fists.' So said the man who had never taken part in any battle.

Events did not go according to King Mpande's wishes. Prince Cetshwayo killed Prince Mbuyazi and was crowned king of the Zulus in 1872.

Mavundla's father was with Cetshwayo's regiment of Usuthu and was killed at the battle of Ndondakusuka, leaving behind his widow and children. Like many survivors of that era, his mother wandered about with her children until she died.

The young Mavundla was rescued by German Lutheran mission priests who took him under their wing, converted him and christened him Stefaan. Mavundla spoke a lot about the desperate state of the Zulu nation, of destitute communities, of people who had reluctantly sought refuge working on the farms in order to have somewhere to lay their heads and have something in their bellies.

He rarely mentioned his misfortunes. He told me how proud he was of me for surviving the hardships I had experienced. He said he would fight day and night to ease the pain that I had endured.

On one occasion Mavundla and I were talking about Langalibalele after reading a newspaper report about his travels overseas to raise money for the school that he was building – Ohlange High – a school that became a beacon of light and learning in Natal and which benefited African students who came from all the corners of the country; a school whose walls still stand proudly in the twenty-first century. As we were talking, Mavundla suddenly became nostalgic and told me that before he met Langalibalele he often felt angry, bitter and helpless about the state of the nation and what had happened to the Zulu people.

He said: 'When Langalibalele Dube came into my life, it was as if the dark cloud that had been hovering over my head all my adult life, had lifted. Like his name, the sun began to shine. Langalibalele said since the nation had suffered at the hands of the invaders, the only thing left for us was to rise and shine, like the sun, and that the only way we could achieve this was through education. Langalibalele's words were, "As a vanquished people, we can only conquer if we acquire education and knowledge. Then we will be on an equal footing with the white man and be able to beat him at his game."'

★

When we arrived at KwaCeza we found a people demoralised. They had just come out of a bloody war between King Dinuzulu and his uncle Zibhebhu. Zibhebhu of course was another of King Cetshwayo's brothers who wanted to be king.

After Cetshwayo had been abducted and effectively deposed, the English had appointed thirteen kinglets to govern the Zulu people, and proclaimed them chiefs. One of these kinglets was Zibhebhu, a brave and skilful fighter who for years had served as a general in one of Cetshwayo's regiments.

The younger Shepstone, whom the Zulu people called Misjan, assisted by Osborne Melmoth, popularly referred to as Malimadi by the locals, apportioned the Nongoma region to Zibhebhu. This region had been King Cetshwayo's stronghold. The Usuthu people lived south-west of the district of Nongoma and to the north-west of the district of Mahlabathini, through which flows the Usuthu River. Mahlabathini was the area which housed King Cetshwayo's palace called Ondini and was approximately forty-five miles to the east of Isandlwana.

Usuthu did not take kindly to being ruled by Zibhebhu particularly because King Cetshwayo's son, Prince Dinuzulu, was alive and under the tutelage of his uncles Ndabuko and Shingana. The people also knew that there was no love lost between Prince Dinuzulu and Zibhebhu as it was strongly rumoured that Zibhebhu had had a hand in the death of King Cetshwayo whom the Zulu people were convinced had been poisoned.

The allocation of this region to Zibhebhu was therefore a sore point with the Usuthu people who had witnessed the Redcoats torch King Cetshwayo's palace at Ondini. They had experienced the humiliating and shameful spectacle of seeing their king, who was powerful both in stature and in physical build, reduced to vagrancy. People were yet to recover from the ordeal of helplessly watching Ondini, the king's palace, which was the hub of activity, civilisation and culture in the area, go up in flames. They were humiliated beyond words. To add pain to their humiliation, they were now to bow down to Zibhebhu, a pill they could not swallow.

The people had loved King Cetshwayo. He had a regal presence unlike his father King Mpande who was of mediocre build and had no claim either to intelligence or charm. King Cetshwayo was majestic. He was tall and extremely dark, very good looking. He was a man of few words. He could wear a haughty look and still look handsome. Apart from his plain-looking father, King Cetshwayo came from a long line of good-looking people. His uncle King Shaka had also been tall. Although not thickset, he was, however, well muscled and imbued with a sense of pride. Shaka's father, King Senzangakhona, was by all accounts good looking. His imbongi, his praise singer, described him as:

> *Obemzimba omuhle nangendlal'enkulu/Endowed with a body that looked*
> *good even during famine*
> *Obebuso bungenandawo yokusolwa/Couldn't find fault with his face*
> *Obemehlo engenandawo yokusolwa/Couldn't find fault with his eyes*
> *Obezandla zingenandawo yokusolwa/Couldn't fault his hands*
> *Obenyawo zingenandawo yokusolwa/Couldn't fault his feet*
> *Obezitho zingenandawo yokusolwa/Couldn't fault his legs*
> *Obesiphundu singenandawo yokusolwa/Couldn't fault the back of his head*

Being the king of the Zulus and a descendant of the house of Senzangakhona, King Cetshwayo was a symbol of power to the Zulu people. At the end of the war between the English and the Zulus, it was most unpalatable and unsightly to the Usuthu people to see their king turned into a felon and having to hide in the mountains.

Even worse, when the Redcoats later hounded the king out of the caves his subjects had to watch helplessly as he was frogmarched to Cape Town. The people responsible for the destruction of their monarch were the same people who had plundered and usurped their land. Now these same people were imposing Zibhebhu, King Cetshwayo's arch enemy, on them. Prince Dinuzulu was still young, a teenager when his father died, and he knew that there was no love lost between his father and his uncle Zibhebhu. He knew that the situation was dire, that it was a case of him having to kill Zibhebhu or be killed by Zibhebhu. His father had warned him about Zibhebhu. When Zibhebhu realised that his nephew was not relenting in the fight to take his rightful place as king, he had enlisted the help of the English to destroy the Mpande bloodline. The English, who had their eye on Zululand, were only too happy to help Zibhebhu kill Dinuzulu who was an obvious impediment to their plans to annex Zululand.

Prince Dinuzulu sought the help of the Boers and they obliged, as usual at a price: they were to be compensated with land. The battle between the prince and his uncle was fought in KwaCeza and concluded in Nongoma at the Indunu (arse) hill, literally behind the town of Nongoma. Somtseu and Osborne Melmoth arrested Prince Dinuzulu in 1889 and banished him to St Helena. He was released in 1898.

★

When I heard of these unholy alliances between Zibhebhu and the English and between the Boers and King Dinuzulu I could not help but recall my experiences of KwaZulu-Natal in the early 1960s when I saw first hand, the cordial relationships between the Zulu people and the Boers in that part of the world.

My parents retired from active service as officers of the Salvation Army in 1959. They left Johannesburg and sought a new home in Hlabisa in Zululand. I went to live with my brother Mzilikazi who was a teacher at Walmansthal Secondary School in Pretoria and I spent my school holidays with my other brother Stanford who was based in Soweto.

I visited my new home for the first time in December 1962. What a culture shock! Although I was from a township with look-alike four-roomed brick houses, where there was no electricity and an outside toilet, Hlabisa was an eyesore. Like most villages in rural areas the homes were mud dwellings. The few brick structures were churches and school buildings, the rest were rondavels and mud huts. There was no electricity, no running water and no toilets.

The first structure that my dad built when he settled there was a pit toilet, much to the wonderment and chagrin of his neighbours. One of them was rumoured to be so taken aback by this building that he went about informing the villagers of the new arrival who had built a house that preserved human excrement. In retrospect, I think he was stirring up the local people to perceive my dad to be a witch.

Being a township girl, with a chip or two on my shoulder, I could not understand or cope with some of the cultural traditions. I could not take the slow pace of life and some of the activities that took place in the village. I found it odd that visitors would enter the house and quietly sit down. They would wait for the people in the house to acknowledge their presence. Where I was from, people greeted as they entered a house – 'Dumelang', 'Sanibonani' and so on. I was also stunned and annoyed by the manner in which young male suitors accosted me. Each time a young man stopped me on the road, the first thing he would say after greeting me would be: 'Uqome phi?' or 'Uthanda phi?' meaning 'who are you dating?' or 'whom do you love?'. I found this question vexing as well as out of line. Most of the time I was tempted to answer, 'That's none of your business.'

But I knew better than to say anything like that.

While I found some of the activities and traditions exasperating, there were some that were downright intriguing and exciting. I enjoyed attending weddings and watching young scantily dressed maidens sing and dance bare-breasted in front of crowds who would in turn adorn the girls by pinning money on the best dancer. There would also be young male dancers dressed in traditional regalia showing off their muscled bodies and doing the indlamu dance of jumping and stamping hard on the ground.

However, what I found most intriguing was the relationship between the locals and the Boers. I was from the township where we did not interact, let alone fraternise with white people. The only white folk we saw in the locations were the policemen, doctors at the clinic and a few priests. The situation was different in Zululand. All the shops were owned by white people. The buses travelling between Mtubatuba and Nongoma belonged to the South African Railways and Harbours and they were driven by Afrikaner men. The ten o'clock bus from Mtubatuba was driven by a colourful Afrikaner who seemed to enjoy engaging and changing gears, going into overdrive as he took on the meandering road. One could hear the sound of the bus approaching kilometres away and whenever school children saw the bus they would shout: 'Thambo Lenyoka, lihlabeli'mzondayo' (snake bone) and the driver would wave at them.

Whenever Father had to travel to Nongoma or Mtubatuba, he would wait for Thambo Lenyoka's driver on the road the day before his trip and inform him of the plan. The next day my dad would be picked up at the gate of our house. The first time I saw the bus making a stop in front of my home to pick my dad up, I was bowled over. Where in the world does one find a white bus driver stopping to pick up a black man in front of his homestead? What also surprised me was to hear the driver refer to my father as 'Mnumzane', mister. That never happened in Johannesburg or in any of the towns I knew. Whites in Johannesburg and Pretoria, the two towns I was familiar with, referred to adult black men as Boy or John. Who in the township would believe this story of a relationship between a Zulu man and an Afrikaner? Wouldn't my father be regarded 'a sell-out' by the township folk who were suspicious of white people, particularly Afrikaners?

219

Years later, my husband and I were involved in a motor car accident on our way to my father's funeral. The accident took place in the early hours of the morning in some forlorn place between Pongola and Nongoma where there was not a hut in sight and no public transport. We were at a loss as to what to do and were waiting for dawn to break when my husband and I were surprised by the appearance, out of nowhere, of a truck driven by a white Afrikaans-speaking man. He stopped and asked what the problem was. Realising that my children seemed more badly injured than I was, he told us to hop onto the truck and he drove us to Benedictine hospital in Nongoma. I was once more astounded by the kindness displayed by an Afrikaner towards a black person.

One day I told Sis Ahh about my observations, and again I was surprised at her answer.

'In the many talks I had with Gogo, not once did she talk ill about the Boers,' Sis Ahh said. 'Apart from the farmer she escaped from, her anger and bitterness were directed at the English. This was in spite of the Blood River massacre, where the Boers killed thousands of Zulu people.'

Grandmother often spoke of Somtseu's shenanigans. Her people had been under the impression that King Cetshwayo and Somtseu were friends and being a friend of the king meant Somtseu would have the interests of the Zulu nation at heart. At the last meeting with Somtseu prior to the outbreak of the war, the Zulu delegation was taken aback by the behaviour of the English delegation. The two groups had held cordial discussions in the morning and were even served lunch. However, after lunch Somtseu and his colleagues told the Zulu delegation to go back and report to the king that he had thirty days to disband his regiments and hand over Mehlokazulu, who murdered his mother, and his father Sihayo, who was King Cetshwayo's general, to the English rulers in Pietermaritzburg to face murder charges. That ultimatum came as a bolt of lightning to the Zulu emissaries.

The people of Zululand knew that during King Dingane's reign and the battle of Blood River, Prince Mpande was taken across the border to be under the protection of the Boers. He was brought back after the war and crowned king of the Zulu people. A few years after King Dinuzulu's return from St Helena Island, he was jailed in Pietermaritzburg for aiding Bhambatha kaMaphisa in the poll tax uprising. It was Prime Minister General Louis Botha who pleaded with the English that King Dinuzulu be released from prison and rather serve his sentence at General Botha's farm in Middelburg. Indeed, King Dinuzulu was released and went to live at the farm in Middelburg until he died in 1913.

The above incidents are but a few examples of British chicanery towards the Zulu people. The old people argue that the Boers did not arbitrarily attack the Zulu people. The Afrikaners negotiated with both King Dingane and his brother King Mpande for land, whereas the English, who were bent on expansionism, did not hesitate to invade Zululand. It was after the Zulus were vanquished that the English turned on the Afrikaners. After the discovery of gold and diamonds in the Orange Free State and the Transvaal the English turned on the Afrikaner in the most cruel ways, including setting up concentration camps during the Boer War for the incarceration of Afrikaner and Zulu women and children. While it would be foolhardy to claim there was a cordial relationship between the Zulus and the Boers, a semblance of respect existed between the two. The Zulus coexisted with the Boers, regarding them as a lesser foe compared to the English who were the common enemy of both the Zulus and the Boers.

★

If I had been sore about the ill-treatment of King Cetshwayo by the English which I had personally witnessed, the people of KwaCeza were sorer about the way the English had treated King Dinuzulu.

I had first-hand experience of the anger and bitterness the people of KwaCeza felt for the foreigners. One day one of the parishioners told me that a resident, uMtwana uMageba, an elderly lady who was one of King Mpande's granddaughters, was dying.

I decided, as a church leader and a member of the community, to visit the sick woman. When I got to her hut, I found there were many local women congregated there. I entered the room where she was lying. When I was announced, the sick woman raised her hand and gesticulated, making a sign that I should leave. At first, nobody understood what the woman was trying to convey. We ignored her as the women in the room made space for me to sit down on the grass mat. The sick woman continued waving her weak hand, telling me to leave. I could no longer ignore her because it had by then become obvious to everyone that I was not welcome at this home. I stood up to leave. As I left the hut one of the woman's middle-aged granddaughters followed me.

When we were out of everyone's earshot, she said: 'Nkosikazi, I hope you will not feel insulted by my grandmother's outburst. It is not personal. It is just that you represent the church, which represents the people who caused her a great deal of pain.'

Trying to conceal the hurt and the tears that were welling in my eyes, I said, 'Yes, I understand.'

'Do you really understand?' she asked. 'If you did, you would not have come to her deathbed. You would have allowed her to die in peace without being reminded of what happened to her uncle and the rest of the nation. Have you ever asked yourself why she has never been to your church? I'll tell you why. The people that you worship are the ones who sent Dinuzulu as a young man to St Helena. She was with him on the island. With other relatives and wives, they were removed from their country and banished to an island. They never enjoyed their youth. Would you forgive such people? Would you?'

'But those were the English people,' I replied. 'My church belongs to the Germans. They had nothing to do with the wars that ravaged our country and brought misery to my people.'

'Oh, you are so naive!' she said. 'So the foreigners whose God you worship are different. They didn't kill us. How different are they from the Boers? You remember Louis Botha? When the English arrested Dinuzulu after the Bhambatha uprising, didn't Louis Botha plead with the English to release him to serve his sentence on his farm? Oh, he was so benevolent. What happened after that? Where are the Boers today? Haven't they teamed up with the English to take our land and rule over us? What happened to Somtseu and King Cetshwayo? Weren't they friends, united against the Boers? Didn't Somtseu ditch Cetshwayo and kill the Zulu people? Go ahead and defend the foreigners as much as you want as long as you stay away from our grandmother. She doesn't deserve to meet her ancestors with the picture of your face in her mind.'

Trying to convert a people whose scars ran so deep was almost impossible. In a way, it reminded me of what happened to my family. I, with my mother and my sister, was forced out of our home to hide in the mountains and when we eventually returned we found that some of our people had capitulated to the whites. I was reminded of the pain and the hurt we suffered listening to my father telling Mother what the English were doing to our king. In retrospect, what Somtseu and Chelmsford did to Cetshwayo paled into insignificance compared with what his son

Dinuzulu and the people of KwaCeza suffered at the hands of Misjan and Malimadi.

The people from KwaCeza and the adjoining areas of Ulundi and Nongoma were not about to forget what the English had done to King Cetshwayo's son, Prince Dinuzulu. It was not as if the Zulu people had not engaged in wars before. The Zulu clans had experienced bloody clashes since time immemorial; the difference was that those wars were fought without foreign interference. For instance, the wars between King Dingiswayo and King Zwide, who at that time was the most feared monarch in Zululand, had been going on for years until King Shaka, who was Dingiswayo's protégé, overpowered King Zwide – a victory which was the precursor to King Shaka's building of the Zulu nation.

In spite of the animosity and the mistrust from some members of our community, Mavundla and I did not give up. In some way, this was poetic justice, for there I was, trying to convert people to a life which I myself had at some stage despised and abhorred. I was now feeding them the same porridge which I had previously refused to swallow.

★

One day, Mavundla was asked to go and pray for a man who was dying. The man was called Cijimpi, because he had belonged to one of King Dinuzulu's regiments. The skinny, grey-haired garrulous old man was popular in the area. Legend was that he had been a warrior during the many skirmishes between Zibhebhu and King Dinuzulu. He lived alone and was often seen seated on top of a huge rock, surveying his cattle and goats while playing his isituruturu, a home-made musical instrument.

When Mavundla got to Cijimpi's house, he was greeted by the usual scene that prevails at a home where death is lurking. The hut where the dying man was lying was full of people. There was a sprinkling of women and many men seated quietly agonising about death. After the customary greetings, the sick man struggled to rise from the grass mat where he was lying. He sat upright and addressed Mavundla.

'Mvangeli, I asked you to come because I need to put something right before I die. As you can see, I am very sick and I don't have long to live. However, before I die, I have to face some home truths. I survived many wars against the foreigners and was abducted by them and forced to live with white people. When the Anglo-Boer War broke out, nkosana, master, tasked me with the duty of hiding the cattle in the mountains. He chose me because I was the only person on the farm who did not have a family, as mine had perished during the war. He took me to the mountain where I lived in a cave looking after the cattle. Occasionally he would come and bring me food and water. I did not like my job but I had no choice. One day, I decided I was going to keep the cows for myself. I waited for nkosana to bring me food. Later that night I left the hideout, taking all the cows with me. I knew it would be days before he discovered I had absconded and taken his cattle with me. I travelled for many days and nights, wandering all over the Zululand plains until I arrived here. I presented myself to the chief and asked for a place to stay and the chief consented. I have lived here all these years and the cows have multiplied. I am now dying and as I have no heir I do not know who to give them to. I have been advised to give them to the church as it is neutral.'

'Why don't you take them back to the owner?' asked Mavundla. 'That would be the right thing to do.'

'First of all, I do not know where he is or whether he is still alive. Secondly, why should I give them back to him? Where did he get these cows from? He was a foreigner in our land – where did he get the cattle from? Didn't the Redcoats kill us and loot our stock?'

'But you said you wanted to put things right. The right thing to do is to send them back to the owner. Surely he can be found,' said Mavundla looking sternly at the man while everybody seemed to hang on every word he uttered.

There was tension in the room. Mavundla knew that everyone was holding their breath in anticipation of what he had to say about the cattle. He knew that the man was dying and wanted to absolve himself from the guilt of theft, but he also knew that there was no way the church could inherit stolen stock. But it was not for him to make a decision that would involve the church.

'I cannot make a decision now. I have to call a meeting with the church elders and tell them of your endowment ...'

Before Mavundla could finish his sentence, one of the men in the hut shook his head and said: 'I don't think it is right for the church to be given the cows. The church is just as guilty of expropriating people's assets as the rest of the foreigners. What we ought to do is to share the cows among ourselves. These cows belong to the Zulu people. No white person brought cattle with them when they arrived in our land. Nor did the church.'

'Elethu.' And so say all of us was the chorus that erupted from the people in the room. They were so animated about the issue of the cattle that they had completely forgotten the reason they were at the old man's house. There was a part of Mavundla that could not believe what he was witnessing. Nor could he understand the behaviour of people squabbling about cattle that did not belong to them in the face of death. Yet at the same time, he could understand the anger and the entitlement these people felt for the cattle. If he had been confronted with this issue twenty years earlier, he probably would also have wanted a share of the loot. However, he now subscribed to Christian values and could therefore not accept what did not belong to him.

In the meantime, the room that had been full of sombre-looking and dignified men was now like a beer hall as everyone shouted at the tops of their voices, arguing about the cattle. During the commotion, the men suddenly bolted out of the hut and went to the kraal where the cattle were. They began helping themselves to the cows. The fact that the owner of the cows was at death's door seemed irrelevant to the men as they fought over the beasts. Nobody wanted to miss out.

When they were done taking the cows, they left Cijimpi to die. The irony is that he didn't die that night. Mavundla, assisted by some of his neighbours, brought him to our house where we looked after him until he died.

Describing the events of that evening to me, Mavundla said: 'Nkosikazi, they divided the cattle among themselves like the Jews helped themselves to Jesus's clothes as he hung on the cross.'

I was now resilient in my resolve to do God's work. I did so by leaning on the wisdom of the scriptures as well as remembering what MaNkosi had taught me about righteousness. I did not always succeed.

Besides preaching the gospel, I organised the local women into groups and taught them cooking, baking and general hygiene. Not everyone appreciated my efforts. The animosity was exacerbated by the fact that

I was an outsider in that community, having come from Dundee. Some villagers would have nothing to do with me or the church. The irony of the situation was that I recognised myself in some of the women who were against Christianity. I recalled that on my return from our sojourn in the mountains I could not have listened to any preacher because I despised the people we called Amakholwa, the believers. I regarded them as cowards and deserters. Oh, how I had loathed them and all that they stood for.

In some respects, my situation was a parody of what my mother and I had lived through. Mother had spent most of her married life alone with us in the caves and dongas while Father was away at Ondini as adviser to the king. I spent most of my married life alone with my children at the church mission.

Mavundla travelled with Langalibalele who was now fondly called 'Mafukuzela'. He had acquired this name because he was constantly on the move, toiling for people who often did not understand his vision which was mainly about opening the eyes of the Zulu people and introducing them to the world of literacy. I never quite appreciated the name Mafukuzela. To me, it sounded like a backhanded compliment as the word somehow depicts a clumsy overburdened traveller or an overworked person. As far as I'm concerned, John Dube had a most gentle demeanour. One couldn't find a more refined or good-mannered man in our region. He was the embodiment of grace and civility. But then I am biased in his favour because he liberated me from illiteracy and probably from a life of celibacy, as I was way over twenty when I met Mavundla. Through Langalibalele I found the good man who became my husband.

As my father had trusted and devoted his life to King Cetshwayo, Mavundla swore by Langalibalele. When Langalibalele was not travelling overseas, he was traversing the length and breadth of Zululand, talking to Amakhosi, the lords, church leaders and teachers about the importance of education.

His newspaper *Ilanga lase Natal* was well established, and now with the many schools that had gone up in Zululand, the people were buying and reading it. Those who could not read, enlisted the help of the neighbours who could, or asked school-going children to read the newspaper to them.

In 1913, King Dinuzulu died in Middelburg in the Transvaal. In 1916 the English installed his son Prince Maphumuzana Solomon to be the paramount chief of the Zulus. They had abolished the use of the title of 'king' by the Zulu people, that 'king' title was now the preserve of the British. Born on St Helena during his father's banishment, King Solomon was the first Zulu king to be given an English name. He was also the first Zulu king to get an education, and the first to be crowned by the white government from Pretoria.

If white people thought that by stripping him of his title and powers, such as banning him from forming regiments and declaring him a chief, the Zulu people would regard him as less than a king, they were mistaken. The people loved, respected and were loyal to him. He also endeared himself to his people by being kind and jovial and he was a colourful personality who enjoyed a good life.

★

With prayer and hard work, we managed to settle in KwaCeza. I was a young bride hoping to create a home for myself and my husband. It wasn't long before I discovered that I was pregnant. When I informed Mavundla that I was in the family way, he was overjoyed at the prospect of being a father. We had to decide where I would have the baby because according to Zulu custom, the first child has to be born at its mother's home so that the young inexperienced woman can be initiated into motherhood by her mother and relatives. Since I didn't have a place called home, the only person I could think of to help me was, without hesitation on my part, MaNkosi. When the time came for me to deliver the baby, Mavundla travelled to Dundee to fetch her so that she could perform the duties of midwife and general overseer. MaNkosi was very happy to see Mavundla and was equally happy that she could be of assistance to us.

My son made his entrance into the world on a cold winter's night. MaNkosi proudly received him, cleaned him up and handed him to me. At that moment I was beside myself with excitement. I, Margaretta, was cradling my son! Who would have thought that the little girl who had lived in caves wearing beads and ibhayi would one day be the proud mother of a son? Who would have thought that one day the girl who had been afraid of sleeping on a bed would cuddle her newborn child, wrapped in warm blankets and comfortably sleeping on a bed? For some strange reason, holding my son in my arms gave me the feeling that I, like everybody else, belonged to this world and that I had a responsibility to raise, nurture and parent a human being. Giving birth to my son liberated me in ways I can never describe. The nagging insecurity that made me feel like a stepchild dissipated. I felt good and whole.

Mavundla had spent the night in the dining room praying. When MaNkosi at last invited him into the bedroom to meet his son, he burst into the room with a big smile. I thought his dimples were even deeper than ever before and his eyes were glowing with love, pride and joy. He ran to my bed and held me tight while looking at his son. Suddenly he let go of me and right there, in the middle of the night, he started prancing and doing the indlamu, the Zulu dance, saying, Ngadla mina, senginomfowethu, ngadla mina. Lucky me, I now have a brother.

He named our son Qholwayo, from the word Qhola, which means something that makes one look or smell good. Ephraim was to be his Christian name. In later years he would be joined by eight siblings.

After the birth of our son, I carried on relentlessly with my duties as the evangelist's wife.

Interestingly, this was also a time in my life when my stature as a Christian woman grew. My faith became stronger by the day and I was now praying with more fervour than I used to. Sometimes I would lose myself in prayer and wouldn't remember what I had been praying about.

The downside to my spiritual growth was that I became ill. Sometimes I feared that I was losing my mind. I hallucinated and went for days without food and water. Many locals put my illness down to an ancestral call to become a sangoma, a traditional spiritual healer. When some congregants approached Mavundla, advising him to allow me to be initiated into ubungoma, he would not hear of it. He told the people they were talking nonsense; that no wife of his was to become a sangoma.

The local people were convinced I was imbued with healing powers. Despite Mavundla's misgivings, sick people were brought to me to pray over and, miraculously, they were cured. A case I recall well and clearly was that of a toddler who was brought to me because she was dying of 'inyoni', a bird. This is a sickness that afflicts small children who suffer from diarrhoea and vomiting resulting in the child's becoming dehydrated. A child suffering from this illness is thought to be bewitched and is usually taken to a medicine person who will give it an enema, which causes further dehydration. Unless taken to a doctor or the hospital where it is put on a drip, the child usually dies.

The child brought to me that day was almost dead. I took one look and saw that the little girl was malnourished and badly in need of fluids. I prayed for her and then made a solution of sugar, salt and boiled water. Using a reed as a straw, I painstakingly fed the liquid to the child.

Reeds were an integral part of rural Zulu life. They had a number of uses, such as providing light in a hut, to administering an enema, that is, transmitting medicine into the bowels. They also formed part of a musical instrument.

Seeing the dire condition of the child, I asked her mother to spend the night at the mission because I wanted to administer the medicine personally. Between the mother and me, and in between prayers, we gave the little girl the solution I had prepared. By morning, the child was blinking. By noon, she had started drinking mahewu.

After that incident, even more sick people were brought to me. I prayed for them and gave them whatever medicine I had in the cupboard. One day they brought a man who had a nasty septic wound on his shin. After praying for him, I carefully washed the wound in water to which I had added a dash of Jeyes fluid. I ground a paste of peach tree leaves and sugar which I smeared on the wound. I told the man to keep the wound clean and continue applying the peach and sugar paste. He came to church a few weeks later, still limping but on the road to restored health.

Most of the sick people were suffering from illnesses caused by mal-nutrition – the result of the poverty that had befallen the nation. After the war, numerous families had been displaced and lost their property, their land and their cattle. There was not enough arable land left for people to grow adequate crops of food. There was famine in the land.

Unfortunately, my ministrations and prayers for the sick did not sit well with some members of the church. Unbeknown to me, I was becoming an embarrassment to the congregation. I had not heard the comments people were making behind my back that I was practising witchcraft under the cloak of Christianity. The white Lutheran bishop summoned Mavundla to his office and told him that my actions were akin to sorcery and had to be stopped.

I couldn't turn people away and I continued giving whatever help I could to the people who still came to me. Mavundla was not pleased that I was disobeying the bishop and the church but I said what I was doing was God's work. I told him that if I was breaking the law, the bishop had every right to have me arrested.

★

In the meantime, Mavundla continued interacting with Langalibalele and travelled all over Zululand with him. One evening Mavundla came back from his travels and meetings, very excited. He told me that the meeting with the chiefs and Langalibalele had been a wonderful success.

Langalibalele had brought along his cousin, Pixley ka Seme. The two men were both from Inanda and, like Langalibalele, Seme was well travelled and highly educated. He was able to plan for action. The two men were a formidable team and they had strong international connections.

They were fortunate to have been born on the right side of the uThukela River. The communities living in this region had embraced Christianity a long while ago. This region was endowed with a number of white liberals such as Bishop Colenso who supported and articulated the African cause. The area had also been privileged in having missionaries who started schools that served the African population. Mavundla and I had grown up on the wrong side of the uThukela River, the Shiyane, Dundee and the Nquthu region, places populated by Boers who were mainly farmers and uneducated.

Mavundla was overawed by the cousins. He said he had, over the years, met many outstanding people but he had never come across anyone as fiery and full of ideas as Seme. Mavundla told me that this Seme fellow had encouraged Langalibalele to continue fostering education, but he had stressed that the main area people should focus on was to bring the various African tribes together and unite them.

Seme told us that the whites had formed a union which excluded us in the land of our forefathers. As Africans we had to come together. An excited Mavundla told me that Seme had said: 'We cannot win the war fighting alone as uZulu. UmZulu, umXhosa and umSuthu must come together.' Mavundla then began singing and prancing about, doing the indlamu, the Zulu dance. Mavundla was a dynamic singer. It wasn't long before the song became a clarion call for the South African Native National Congress.

MuZulu, MuXhosa, MuSuthu, MuVenda hlanganani
Zulus, Xhosas, BaSotho and BaVenda come together

Mavundla's absences from the mission and his alliance with Langalibalele did not go unnoticed by the church, members of the congregation as well as some members of the community. They were aware that he was travelling with Mafukuzela, persuading the people to come together to oppose the whites. On Sundays when he was present in church, his sermon was always punctuated with the mention of current events. At the end of his oration he would ask the congregation to pray for King Solomon 'who has been rendered impotent by the English'. He would also ask the congregation to 'pray for the nation to be strong and not to give up'. Some members of the church supported his actions while others harboured mixed feelings about the inclusion of politics in the church. Some congregants who had given up fighting oppression were not impressed. They argued that what he and Mafukuzela were engaged in was a futile exercise; they were convinced that the 'crazy pair' (as some of the locals referred to them) were living in a dream world if they thought they could overthrow the whites.

One day a delegation from the Lutheran Church led by the bishop himself visited us. The head of the church told Mavundla that they understood his involvement in Zulu politics. Having said that, they then told him the church wasn't paying him to work for Mafukuzela, that he was working for the church. Then the famous word came up, the word that Somtseu and Chelmsford and all those in power had so often used in the past – an ultimatum. Mavundla was given an ultimatum to choose between the church and Mafukuzela. He had a month in which to respond.

By then we had four young children and were living on church property. Our lives were entirely tied to the mission. Our children were attending the mission school. We had nothing of our own, not even a 'bankstool', a bench made out of cheap wood. Unlike Langalibalele and Seme who had superior educations and were from wealthy families, Mavundla and I had no safety net. Without a profession or skills, we were beholden to the church.

In the meantime, Seme and Dube travelled all over South Africa. They had been joined by other educated Africans such as Montsioa and Ma'am Maxeke. The local newspaper *The Natal Witness*, carried articles about 'restless natives' in an attempt to demonise and trivialise the move by Africans to unite against white oppression.

In spite of the negative publicity, the momentum to start an organisation that would bind all Africans was growing. Everyone was talking about imbumba, the coming together. The 'MuZulu, MuXhoza, MuSuthu and MuVenda hlanganani' ditty was heard in the valleys and on the pathways, at church meetings and revivals. There was hope in the land. Africans seemed poised to rise from the ashes of defeat in the hope of charting a new life.

For Mavundla and our family, life was about to take a different turn. We were troubled by the decision we were forced to take. It seemed unfair for the church to expect us to choose sides. I even started to accept how correct the young woman had been, years back, when she told me I was naive. How could I not have seen what the white people's game was? White people, whether Christians or not, were united against us. The young woman who had chastised me when I visited her dying grandmother had been right. I had been stupid not to see what seemed to be clear to everyone.

The church awaited our response. Mavundla spent sleepless nights trying to decide what to do. He needed to confer with Langalibalele but we did not know where he was. He could be anywhere, overseas on a fund-raising trip, or even somewhere in the country. Nor did we know Seme's whereabouts. And time was running out for us.

One evening after prayer and after tucking the children into bed, Mavundla said to me: 'Nkosikazi, I have reached my decision. I am going to tell the church that I am no longer going to be with Langalibalele, that from now on I shall concentrate on the work of the church. But first, I have to inform Langalibalele, then I shall talk to the church elders.'

'What reasons are you going to give to Langalibalele for turning against him?' I asked.

'I am not turning against him. I am choosing to stay with the church and with my family. If I choose to work for the nation, I run the risk of being homeless. I grew up without a home. I am not prepared to let my children be drifters like I was. I have to stop the cycle of homelessness.'

In the days that followed, I noticed that the decision not to be with Dube had taken its toll on Mavundla but I didn't realise how badly he had been affected by this impasse. Not long after he informed me of his decision, Mavundla became sick and had to be rushed to KwaCeza hospital where he was diagnosed as having suffered a stroke. He was kept in hospital for some weeks, something that worked in our favour for it bought us some time for our response to the church.

Langalibalele heard of Mavundla's illness and visited him in hospital. At first Mavundla did not take Langalibalele into his confidence. Being the intelligent man he was and furthermore as an old friend, Langali-

237

balele questioned Mavundla on what could have triggered the stroke, insisting that something must have been bothering him. Mavundla ended up telling him about the church's ultimatum and the decision he had made. He told him he was aggrieved by the fact that he could no longer be part of the canvassing.

Langalibalele told Mavundla not to be sorry for the decision he had taken as he had done commendable work bringing people together to fight oppression.

He said, 'Without you, I would not have been so readily accepted by the people of this region. You have done a great job. Sometimes one has to make unpalatable choices. You have a family to look after. Part of our work is to ensure that the African family stays intact. You stay with the church and continue doing church work, preaching about love and morality and Christian values. This community needs you and it does not mean that you are no longer one of us. Seme and I will keep you posted about the progress of the organisation and of the nation.'

When Mavundla was discharged from hospital, he went back to the mission to continue with church duties. He informed the church of his decision to choose the church above politics. Everybody was happy. His illness, however, was a wake-up call for us. We realised that we needed to have a place of our own. We could not live on the church property for ever. Without notifying the church, Mavundla privately approached the Inkosi from the neighbouring village of IsiKhwebezi and asked for land. The Inkosi allowed him to settle on his land and with the help of our sons, Qholwayo and Johannes, he built our own home so that by the time we retired, we would be able to move to our homestead at IsiKhwebezi.

Reacting to the white people's decision to form the Union of South Africa, Langalibalele and Africans from all over the country met in Bloemfontein in 1912 to form the South African Native National Congress. John Langalibalele Mafukuzela Dube was elected president of the organisation. It was with great sadness that Mavundla could not attend, but he did ask the congregation to pray for the success of the conference. Not once did he voice his pain of not being able to attend the meeting of the organisation he had put so much effort into building. I could see that he was hurting and when I asked him if he regretted not being able to attend the conference, his answer was: 'Did Moses reach the promised land?'

He kept himself informed by reading newspaper reports that carried articles about the meeting. As the delegates from our region came back from the conference, Mavundla was on his horse visiting them to learn more about the proceedings. He expressed disappointment that Langalibalele had been elected president. He had harboured hopes that Pixley ka Seme would have been the choice for the position. However, that did not mean he had no confidence in Langalibalele, nor did it mean his regard and respect for Langalibalele had been eclipsed by Seme.

'You see, Nkosikazi, Langalibalele is a Christian gentleman and a doer of things. Whereas Seme is more of an orator; he is someone who will move the people. That is why I think he would have been the best choice.'

I didn't quite get what Mavundla meant because I had seen Langalibalele in action. He had been responsible for so much progress in Dundee that I battled to understand my husband. Of course there were many instances where he was much ahead of my thinking, particularly when it came to political issues. I admired both Langalibalele and Seme and was happy that one of them had been elected to the position. Obviously Mavundla didn't think so.

★

We continued to get news about Mafukuzela. He was travelling all over the world. The school he had built in Inanda, the Ohlange Institute, was doing well. Two of our children were students there. The newspaper *Ilanga lase Natal* remained successful, continuing to inform the Zulu people about current affairs. By now Mafukuzela was no longer the president of the African National Congress, as the South African Native National Congress had been renamed. It was rumoured that he had disgraced himself by collaborating with white people. This rumour was most depressing to Mavundla who continued to idolise Langalibalele. We were now retired and lived in IsiKhwebezi, but Mavundla's health was deteriorating.

One day we read in *Ilanga* that Langalibalele was sick and had been admitted to the King George V hospital in Durban. Mavundla expressed a desire to visit him there. I realised that he was in no condition to travel alone and so I offered to accompany him to Durban. I had never travelled anywhere before. I had never been in a bus, let alone a train. My experience of getting from one place to another, except of course on foot, was limited to the conveyance in which the old man had fetched my mother and her daughters to take us to Oubaas's farm, and the cart in which the two kind men had taken me to the mission school when I was escaping from the farm. Since then I had not even been to Nongoma or Mahlabathini. Nor had I ever been to shops. As a minister's wife, I led a protected life. Mavundla was the one who travelled and brought home whatever we needed. I was in my sixties, a grandmother, and my children were scattered all over the world.

We had to decide which route to use to get to Durban. We could go via Dundee, pass Blood River, Rorke's Drift and the uMzinyathi River. Clearly, that would have been a trip down memory lane and Mavundla suggested it as such. He was hoping I would find closure to my past. But I was opposed to the idea. I wanted to let sleeping dogs lie. He relented and we travelled to Durban via Melmoth and Eshowe.

I couldn't go to Durban by horse cart; those days were gone for ever. When I got into the bus and it began moving I immediately felt sick. Realising that I was about to throw up, Mavundla opened the window to let in fresh air. But once he did that, the dust came gushing in as we were travelling on a dirt road. Fortunately it didn't take long for the feeling of nausea to subside which allowed me to enjoy the rest of the journey. I marvelled at the sight of trees and houses as they moved backwards. It didn't occur to me that it was the bus that was moving away and not the trees.

We were met in Durban by Evangelist Buthelezi who offered to take us to the hospital, but first we had to go to his house in Chesterville township to freshen up. Durban was a strange place. For the first time in my life I saw crowds at the train station, multitudes of people occupying a single space. They looked like ants moving in all directions. I had never seen anything like it.

The town was a further revelation. The roads were broad and people drove cars as though it was an easy mission. Then there were the rickshaws in their colourful outfits and heavily decorated wagons. They went up and down the city streets carrying passengers, running as though the weight on their backs was nothing. I was intrigued by the sight of African women carrying bundles on their heads. When I enquired about the bundles I was told that the women did laundry for white people and they were taking the washed articles back to their employers.

I was fascinated by the young African women walking along the streets wearing high heels and tight-fitting skirts. Some were in the company of men dressed in baggy suits topped with wide-brimmed hats. They looked majestic and yet very un-Zulu; they moved about without a stick and seemed carefree. They were so different and lived in another world from us people from KwaCeza or IsiKhwebezi.

The hospital visiting hours were in the afternoon which was why Buthelezi suggested we should go to his house in Chesterville Township to freshen up and have something to eat before we went there. Nobody had warned me about what a township looked like. This location was built high up on a scenic mountainside and climbing the stairs that connected the streets was arduous. By the time we got to Buthelezi's house I was quite out of breath. The houses were so close to each other that I was sure one could hear someone coughing in the next house.

I was most uncomfortable. I couldn't understand how people could live so close to others. When the government began apportioning morgen to us in IsiKhwebezi we had felt crowded and feared we would suffer from claustrophobia, and yet that was nothing compared to the closeness of the houses in the township. We freshened up, using the shower that each family unit had which was built outside the house. We had lunch and got ready to go to the hospital.

We travelled to the hospital in the afternoon where I met MaKhumalo, Langalibalele's wife, for the first time. She embraced us and told us that she had heard a great deal about us and she was pleased that we had managed to come and see her husband.

She led us into the ward where Langalibalele lay attached to many gadgets and machines. Although he was unable to speak, he smiled when he saw us. We hadn't seen him for more than three decades and, like us, he had aged. He had gone bald and his skin looked grey. But he still looked distinguished, even on his sick bed. There were many people coming in and out of his ward. Some of them knew Mavundla and they talked animatedly to him, asking him about the situation in Northern Zululand. Most of the people we met were from the townships and were concerned about the effects of the homeland system on the lives of the people.

We stayed in Durban for a week as guests of the Reverend Buthelezi. Apart from visiting the hospital daily, Mavundla took me shopping and showed me the many sights of Durban, places I had only heard people speak about. Buthelezi took us to Stanger and showed us the famous promontory known as Shaka's Rock. He also took us to Pietermaritzburg and I was able to see various government buildings and the jail where many of my people were incarcerated.

On the afternoon of our departure, I saw Langalibalele smile as Mavundla bade him goodbye. He watched Mavundla as he left his bedside, his eyes following him all the way out of the ward. It was as though he knew that they would never see each other again, that together they had reached the end of an era.

We left Durban with heavy hearts. On our way home Mavundla bemoaned the fact that there was so much he wanted to talk to Langalibalele about but couldn't because Langalibalele was too ill. In 1946 John Mafukuzela Langalibalele Dube died at his home in Inanda. Mavundla was distraught. For the Mavundla family, it was like the little light that had been flickering on a reed had been blown out.

★

Mavundla's health deteriorated after Langalibalele's death, and we were on our own. Our children were married and scattered all over the country. My oldest son Qholwayo who had established himself as a businessman in KwaHlabisa, decided to move us from IsiKhwebezi to his place in KwaHlabisa so that he could take care of his father.

This time I was on the road as a grandmother and I was going to be received by my daughter-in-law MaMhlongo who welcomed us and made our lives as comfortable as she could. Although Mavundla put up a brave front, I could see that he was nearing the end of his journey. One morning I woke up and, as was our habit, I got out of bed and knelt down to pray. I called out his name. 'Mavundla, morning has broken. Let us thank the Lord for the mercy of seeing another day,' I said.

There was no response from him. I rose from my kneeling position and went over to his bed. One look at his face and I knew he was no longer with us. He had died peacefully during the night. He went off like the gentleman he was. He was not going to disturb me and the grandchildren. When I looked at him, he looked so much at peace. It was as though he was enjoying a trouble-free slumber. He was free of the aches that had been bothering him.

I cannot fully remember his funeral because everything happened as if in a dream. Many people attended, coming from as far afield as Durban and Johannesburg. Some were old acquaintances from the church, others were people he had been working with when he was campaigning with Langalibalele.

It was only after his burial that I was able to retrace my life and put it into perspective. I started to piece together the puzzle of my life and to realise that I had come full circle.

I was now living in Hlabisa, a region that was dominated by the descendants of Ngebeza who took me and my mother and sister into their fold when we were vagrants who had been hiding in the mountains. My life began as an African who believed devoutly in the power of my ancestors. It will end with me being a Christian, believing in the power of Jesus.

I have many questions that I have no answers for, and I have real regrets, yet I have had many blessings to be thankful for. I was married to the most reasonable and loving man a woman could hope to find. Together we had enjoyed a fruitful life full of love and joy. We had been blessed with nine children, five boys and four girls. I was surrounded by many grandchildren and did not want for anything. Still, hardly a day passed without me wondering about my mother and sister and their lives. To this day, I feel guilty for leaving them behind but I would do it again as there was nothing else I could do other than stay on and suffer undoubtedly dire consequences, which most likely would have extended to them as well.

People often shower me with praise for surviving my ordeal. Although I was lucky to get away, and can rationalise my actions, the guilt has left a hole in my heart, an emptiness which I will carry to my grave.

One true consolation I have about my life is that although I witnessed a great deal of unwarranted waste of lives, I am proud to say I come from a stock of people who fought gallantly to save their land. There are those who will argue it was a futile exercise because the odds were stacked against the Zulus. For me, it is with a deep sense of pride to know that our regiments gave it their all.

Epilogue

One day Sis Ahh and I decided to visit the Mavundla graves at Gwegwede next to Hlabisa where Gogo and her husband, as well as some of her children, lie buried. The graves are in an overgrown piece of ground near the Mavundla home-stead. We had visited the graves many times before, but as we wrapped up the writing of the book, I was seized with the urge to go back to the burial grounds, to be in the presence of my ancestors.

We arrived at the graveyard around noon under a blistering sun. Sis Ahh cleared space on top of Gogo's grave, put her walking stick down and sat on the big boulders encircling the grave. I looked around, nursing my fear of snakes, and thought, 'Trust her, the stoic woman, to sit down at such a place.' I was standing next to the grave surrounded by grass that was up to my knees, amid old trees and shrubs that had stood around the graves for years posing as sentinels. Although the branches of the trees were laden with birds' nests, strangely there was not a bird in sight. It was tranquil. Occasionally a lizard would slither quickly past our feet and I would jump, thinking it was a snake.

'Gogo died in 1962 while Mother was away in Johannesburg being midwife to Sis B – Beatrice – who was giving birth to her first child,' said Sis Ahh. 'I received a message from Uncle Qholwayo saying Gogo was at death's door and she was asking for mother. So Uncle decided I should come over and stand in

247

Mother's place to assuage the dying lady. I was not sure if I would be able to stand the pain of watching the woman who raised me leave this world. To my relief, Gogo told me that she was not sick. She was tired.

'The first thing that struck me when I entered Gogo's bedroom was that she was not lying on her bed. She was sleeping on the grass mat. I asked my uncle's wife why Gogo was not on her bed. She told me that Gogo had insisted on lying on the grass mat. To me, this was a bad omen. It was an indication that she was embarking on her new journey. She was, after all, an old woman who was at the end of her life.

'When I decided to visit Gogo, I wasn't sure how lucid she was and when I entered her hut I was surprised that she recognised me. She lifted her head and said: "So you are here, and as usual my daughter is away visiting her children in the city. I wanted to talk to her before I go."

'"Where are you going Gogo?" I asked.

'"I am going to the Shiyane mountains. I have not seen my father and grand-mother in a while. I have to be with them. I know I've not been to that part of the country in years and I fear I may get lost but I know my people will come and meet me on the way; after all, they have been beckoning me to come over. I have told them I am coming. I am now ready to go. I have seen my mother and my father and I told them I would be with them soon. Mzukulu, grandchild, I have to go now."'

She died a few days later on the same day that one of her granddaughters, my sister B, gave birth to a baby girl who was named Seloane, a lament.

'I found the death of Gogo and the birth of the little girl symbolic,' said Sis Ahh. 'Only Gogo could make such an exit — departing from this world at the same time as one of her granddaughters brings a child into the world. To me it was

too much of a coincidence. She was gone. She had ultimately left to join her father and her grandmother and all the members of the Makhoba family who had since departed from this world. The girl who had braved the harsh Zulu environment and survived the cruelty of the English soldiers was no more.'

Historical Note

When the Boers in the Transvaal and the English came together to form the Union of South Africa in 1910, a union that excluded Africans, the scramble for land was in full force. Gold and diamonds had been discovered in Kimberley and Johannesburg and cities were sprouting all over the country. White people grabbed more and more land and those who were not into mining were into farming. The English, Boers and Germans were doing a roaring business feeding the nation.

The Bhambatha uprising having failed, the white people were now free to enforce the law obliging African men to carry a pass book and to pay poll tax. Black people lived off the land more or less as subsistence farmers. There were no surplus supplies from the sale of which they could have earned money.

Many able-bodied men left the rural areas for the cities to earn the money to pay this tax. The most favoured route out of the impasse of paying the tax was to find employment on the gold and diamond mines in Johannesburg and Kimberley. The mines were recruiting through TEBA – The Employment Bureau of Africa which had a slogan that read: 'Join TEBA indlela elula yokuya eGoli', the easy way to go to Johannesburg, the City of Gold. The large poster that was prominently displayed at leading local stores lured many young men who thought TEBA was indeed the easy way to go.

These recruits soon realised that the way to eGoli, to Johannesburg, was far from easy. Together with recruits from other parts of the country, they were taken in large numbers and thrown into train carriages to be transported to the mining towns. There they soon discovered that there was nothing glamorous about working in the mines. Each day meant plunging into the belly of the earth, like being buried alive, an aspect they had not been warned of or prepared for by the recruiting officials.

By this time the white government, made up of the English and the Boers (who were no longer referred to as Boers but as Afrikaners), had thoroughly entrenched itself. A parliament set up in Cape Town was passing many laws that made the lives of Africans more difficult by the day. The worst of these laws was the introduction of the pass book for African men, a book that controlled the movements of black people. Failure to produce a pass on demand was a criminal offence which carried a jail sentence.

Later, when the National Party government came to power in 1948 the policy of separate development, better known to the world as apartheid, and the homeland system were introduced. This brought about what was termed the 'consolidation of black spots'. It resulted in blacks being forcibly removed from fertile areas and transported to large settlements in remote and barren parts of Northern Zululand. There were mass removals of Africans from areas such as Roosboom and Ekuphumleni in Ladysmith to Ezakheni; black people from the Washbank area were moved to the Limehill complex near Dundee. It was during this era that the white government tried to justify its 'separate but equal' theory by introducing what they called 'physical planning' which saw the apportioning of land to black families in fractions of morgen – a morgen is approximately two acres. Men, women and children were carted with their belongings on government trucks to be settled in new and unfamiliar environments. Some of the people who were relocated in fact held freehold title deeds, proving their ownership of the land.

Each family that was moved to these new areas was allotted a quarter of a morgen for a homestead and one morgen of arable land for subsistence farming. Grazing was allocated communally per clan. For a people whose existence was based on farming vast tracts of land to be reduced to eking out a living on a smallholding, the loss of what had been their own land was a bitter pill to swallow.

Magistrates were appointed to administer these areas with the help of chiefs who were also appointed by the government. The role of the chiefs was to be the government's caretakers, to settle petty squabbles between members of the community and apportion land for farming. Major felonies and crimes were handled by the state police and the magistrates. Although the king received a minuscule allowance from the government, he played no role in the day-to-day lives of the Zulu people. He was a ceremonial figure, invited to cut ribbons at the opening of new buildings.

This movement saw the desertion of many Africans who had settled on white farms. The farm system dictated that they work on the farm for six months to earn the right to till the land for their own benefit as well as keep a few head of cattle on the white farmer's land. They, too, of their own volition, trekked in droves to seek refuge in areas of Amakhosi after breaching the conditions of their stay on the farms. Some families were evicted from the farms because, possibly, one of the sons had not abided by the farmer's conditions, and had joined TEBA rather than staying there.

In 1952, the government introduced passes for women. African women had to apply for a reference book. Local indunas called meetings to tell women that they now had to get reference books like their husbands and sons, and that this was so that they could qualify for the government grant that was paid out every second month. Indunas advised women to be prepared for the government officials who would be coming to take their photographs and fill in their details. Women were not given the option or opportunity to refuse or to consider whether or not they wanted to carry the passes.

On the day the government officials arrived women had to present themselves at their local magistrate's court where, one by one, like lambs in a slaughter house, they posed for the cameras. They were told to remove their head scarves and not to smile for the camera. Old women had to remove their headgear and expose their grey hair. The white people taking the photographs seemed oblivious of the fact that elderly Zulu women never appeared in public without some covering on their heads. What if any of their sons-in-law walked past and saw them without a scarf on their heads? The officials informed the women that they should carry the books at all times. They had a little pouch with a string so that they could be hung around the neck.

There was strong resistance to the imposition of passes on women which culminated in the women's anti-pass protest march to Pretoria led by the African National Congress Women's League on 9 August

1956. But it was to no avail. With the homeland plan in place, and African men having acclimatised to carrying the pass book and producing it on demand, the government's next move was to insist that African women carry passes.

The law requiring the possession of pass books for Africans in South Africa was finally repealed in 1986.

OkaMakhoba's reference book, issued in 1957
— the only photograph of Gogo in existence

Glossary and Guide to Zulu Words and Phrases

Abakhephehleli – Self-styled warriors who tried to maintain Zulu culture and traditions after the white government did away with the king's regiments. These young men from various regions challenged each other and engaged in mock stick fights. Sometimes these competitions ended with a few deaths. They also entertained crowds with their dancing. They were anti-religion and averse to education

abantwana – The word means 'children'; umntwana is a child. In Zululand members of the royal family are referred to as Abantwana, children

Amabhinca – Name given by Amakholwa to Zulu people who continued their traditional way of life and did not convert to Christianity or the ways of white people

amadumbe – Popular Zulu vegetable which is a cross between a potato and a yam

Amakholwa – 'The believers'. Zulu people who adopted Christianity and the ways of white people

Anglo-Boer War – Conflict between the British and the Boers in the Transvaal Republic and the Orange Free State, 1899-1902. Also known as the Second Boer War or the South African War

Anglo-Zulu War – Conflict between the British Empire and the Zulu Kingdom, January to July 1879

bayede, wena wendlovu – Salutation to the king

dagga – Cannabis, marijuana

ibhayi – Zulu women tied a loin cloth around their necks as apparel to cover their bodies. This was partly because the skirt underneath the ibhayi was short and married women had to cover their bodies. The garment covered them from the neck to below the knee and was made out of animal skin. Later, European traders introduced loin cloths made out of cotton. Unlike women from other African countries whose loin cloths have colourful designs, Zulu women's ibhayi are of plain colours, some bordered with colourful beads. The plural form is mabhayi

ibheshu – The apron worn by men that covers their front and back. It is made out of animal hide. An ibheshu covers the buttocks and beneath it was iqoyi or inkamanga which served as underpants. To this day, some Zulu men wear the ibheshu at traditional weddings or celebrations

ihlala – A wild fruit also known as a monkey apple. It is as big as a tennis ball, has slippery pips and may be very sweet. The plural form is amahlala

ilima – An African tradition whereby the community pools its resources to assist a family perform a much-needed task, such as building a hut or kraal or hoeing a field

imbenge – A saucer-like container made out of grass and usually used to cover a beer pot

imbizo – A meeting

imbuya – Wild green vegetable that resembles miniature spinach

indlamu – A Zulu dance

indoni – A dark, sweet-tasting grape-like fruit that grows along river banks. Sometimes a woman's complexion is described as 'dark as an indoni'

induna – A headman or councillor in traditional Zulu society

inhloko – This was a cone-shaped headgear sewn on married women's hair and polished with red ochre. This is another item that has found its way into modern African women's fashion. South African women from various ethnic groups wear this headgear at weddings or traditional celebrations

intombazane – A young girl

intombi – A grown woman

inyanga – A herbalist

iqhikiza – A grown-up woman, usually past marriageable age (or a woman 'on the shelf'). She is usually in charge of young maidens to make sure that they do not stray from the straight and narrow. She imparts wisdom to the young women on how to behave, what to look for in a man, how not to allow a boy to penetrate her sexually. She is a respected member of the community and the boys and men hold her in high esteem. In short, she is part of the Zulu system of governance

isicholo – Another name for inhloko

isicoco – The black ring headdress that looks like rubber, worn by outstanding warriors. It was also awarded to married men

isidwaba – This was a pleated skirt made out of hide. The animal skin was soaked in fats (oils) and crushed for days, resulting in a soft leather-like chamois. The present-day trend is for African women, both rural and from the townships, to attend weddings wearing the modern isidwaba made of cloth and decorated with beads, with the ibhayi thrown over the shoulders

isigqiki – A chair carved out of the trunk of a tree in such a manner as to provide a seat for a king or mnumzane (see below). Women did not sit on an isigqiki; they sat on a grass mat. It could also be used by both men and women as a head rest or pillow

isilo samabandla – The title for the Zulu king

isituruturu (isitolotolo) – A musical instrument that vibrates

ithunduluka – A wild orange-red coloured fruit, a little sour in taste

Jantoni – John Dunn, adviser to King Cetshwayo who re-joined the British during the Anglo-Zulu War

kaffir – A derogatory, offensive term for a black person

knobkerrie – A short stick with a knob at the end, traditionally used as a weapon

lobola – Payment of goods, cattle or money by an African bridegroom to the parent or guardian of his bride; sometimes referred to as 'bride-wealth'

mahewu – Traditional non-alcoholic southern African drink made from fermented maize meal

mnumzane – Mister

muthi – Could be a concoction of herbs used for the treatment of various ailments, imaginary or real. Usually dispensed by an inyanga or a sangoma. It could also be a love potion

mvangeli – Head of the church. Although the word has its origins in 'evangelist', African evangelists of earlier times were not of the Billy Graham type. They did not go about spreading the scriptures but were confined to their churches

mzala – Cousin

ngadla mina – Literally means 'I eat', but it is a war cry. When a warrior plunged a spear into the enemy's body, he would say 'ngadla mina', as if to say 'I've got you'. The same phrase is used as a self-congratulatory utterance. For instance, when informed that he is top of the class in a particular subject, a student would say 'ngadla mina'. It is important to note that the phrase is uttered when in company of others; it's like saying 'eat your heart out'. A similar phrase, wadla wena, may be used by spectators at a competition; in English one would say 'you go, girl/ boy'. (See also ucu)

nkosazana – An unmarried woman. However, during colonial times young unmarried white women were referred to as nkosazana, while white unmarried men were called nkosana

onongqayi – A policeman

phutu – Mealie meal porridge

praise singer – In traditional African society, a composer and orator of poems praising a chief or other figurehead (imbongi)

sangoma – A diviner

sawubona – Good day

sjambok – A long stiff whip, originally made from rhinoceros hide

ubuhlalu – Colourful beads that were used to adorn people's bodies. Different colours were used to denote different regions. Beads were first introduced into Zululand by Arab traders and later used by the Portuguese who colonised present-day Mozambique. Young maidens who were virgins were not allowed to wear beads of any colour but white

ucu – A string of beads. Young maidens offered ucu to a man to indicate that they were in love with him. A maiden would also give ucu to her suitor as a sign that she accepts his marriage proposal. On receiving ucu from a maiden, the man would jump high in the air and perform a dance and say 'ngadla mina'

udiwo – A clay calabash. Izindiwo is the plural

ukungena – A Zulu custom whereby a man marries his brother's (or other relative's) widow for the purpose of continuing his brother's/relative's lineage and providing their family with sustenance. It is not compulsory but subject to negotiation between the widow and her brother-in-law and the family

ukusoma – Sex without penetration

umakhweyana – A Zulu musical instrument along the lines of a violin

umcaba – Dry ground sorghum

umfazi – Wife. In today's parlance, the word umfazi is hardly ever used, except in expression of anger or when one is being derogatory towards women

umgcagco – A traditional Zulu wedding

umgwaqo – A road, not a footpath

uMvelinqangi – The Creator whom the Zulu people worshipped and revered

uNdlunkulu – All the king's wives are oNdlunkulu. It is only the queen mother who is referred to differently as Indlovukazi. It does not have to be the first wife. There will be factors that qualify her as Indlovukazi, such as if she is the daughter of another king. The king's first wife, usually a princess, is the one who lays down the law for other women in the royal palace

uNkosikazi – Wife. This term was used mainly by Christians as opposed to the use of the word umfazi that was used by traditional Zulus

uZibandlela – The month of December (lit. 'the covered pathways')

Acknowledgements

Apart from my sister Ahh and cousin Mjabhi, and Rachel Browne - the first person I discussed the book with, I am indebted to many people who made it possible for me not only to write this book but exposed me to the painful history of the Zulu people. My daughter Sibongile and her husband Thibeli, my son Pelo and his wife Motlalepula for their financial support, footing my travelling bill. Thibeli gets special thanks for helping me with the laptop as I am what township youth refers to as a BBT (born before technology). Thanks also to my first child Thulisile who feels very strongly about Zulu culture. And of course my two partners in crime, Antjie Viedge, a retired advocate, and her husband Ingo, who went over the manuscript with a fine toothcomb, making sure I did not misrepresent anyone. My friend, Cathy van Nieuwkerk, who agonised with me over many cups of tea, when publishers rejected my manuscript, as well as my friend Pauline Gule who read the first draft of the manuscript.

As for my siblings, my brother Professor Mzilikazi Khumalo and his wife Rose, my sisters Sis B, Catherine, and the twins Thandi and Nomsa were my sounding board and had to listen to the story of Grandma even at times when they least wanted to hear it. I recall how Nomsa would say: 'Uyabhora,' meaning I was becoming a bore because I kept telling them about my latest find, or asking them questions related to the book. Mzilikazi, in his authoritative style of talking would simply say: 'How far are you now? You must get on with it, that book is long overdue.'

What I know about Zulu people's lifestyle I got from Professor Themba Msimang. I take my hat off to him for the way he held my hand in the early days of writing this book. He led me, a township girl, through the cultural dongas, mountains and the pathways of Zululand to understand what life was like in the days of old. Ume nje, Thabizolo!

My dear sister-in-law and friend Doris Khumalo from Westville in Durban and her sister Professor Phyllis Zungu were useful crutches I leaned on when confusion and ignorance about matters pertaining to the Zulu people would seem to get me down. Professor Zungu, a respected academic and leading anthropologist, was a great source of information and clarity. With the numerous contacts she has at the university and the vast Zulu community she is involved with, there was never a time when I asked her for help and came back empty-handed. Thanks bo Dlungwana.

Professor RS Khumalo of the University of KwaZulu-Natal and author of the John Langalibalele Dube biography was able to fit me into his busy schedule and travels between airports. RS renders the Khumalo clan respectability and we are greatly indebted to him and his numerous intellectual endeavours that continue to place the Khumalos in the limelight. Then there is the forever dependable Zakhele Khumalo whose knowledge of the Zulu people is beyond reproach. I would call him at the dead of night asking for help and not once did he lose his temper; instead he would say: 'Umsebenzi wasekhaya,' meaning I am doing this for the family. Mashobane!

My research offered me an opportunity to interact with many ordinary Zulu men and women who were more than eager to share whatever stories they knew. One of the women who stands out is Mbili Ngubane from Rorke's Drift who would become so animated in her narrations that I often had to rein her in, reminding her that I was mainly interested in the 'Redcoats' stories. No writer interested in that part of the world should miss talking to her. She is history personified. The sad reality is that all the information she has will die with her.

To the Mavundlas, my maternal relatives who spurred me on and told me I owed it to them to write the book, I am proud that I am part of you. One outstanding couple in this equation is Khulile Mavundla and her husband Lunga Gcabashe. Their home was my hotel and my office. Kwande bo Lamula.

And last but not least, to the Bookstorm editorial crowd. I am grateful that you believed in me, particularly the venerate trio of Louise Grantham, Nicola van Rooyen and Russell Clarke (a tireless editor and critic). To my editor, Pam Thornley, for doing what I thought would be impossible – merging Ahh's voice and my own to make this a book worth reading. Give that woman a Bell's!

To the ones I've not mentioned, you know who you are and I know some of you will give me a tongue lashing for the oversight. I swear I am not being malicious. I will make it up to you somehow. In the meantime, spend some time with OkaMakhoba on her journey through life. Believe me, revisiting her journey has humbled me in ways I cannot express.

Nomavenda C Khumalo Mathiane
Granddaughter
Johannesburg, 2016

CPSIA information can be obtained
at www.ICGtesting.com
Printed in the USA
LVOW10s0959060517
533492LV00002B/3/P